Understanding Infant Development

Understanding Infant Development

Margaret B. Puckett & Janet K. Black

with Joseph M. Moriarity

Redleaf Press
www.redleafpress.org
800-423-8309

Published by Redleaf Press
a division of Resources for Child Caring
10 Yorkton Court
St. Paul, MN 55117
Visit us online at www.redleafpress.org.

First edition 2007
Interior typeset in Janson Text
Interior illustrations by Chris Wold Dyrud
Printed in Canada
14 13 12 11 10 09 08 07   1 2 3 4 5 6 7 8

Redleaf Press books are available at a special discount when purchased in bulk for special premiums and sales promotions. For details, contact the sales manager at 800-423-8309.

Library of Congress Cataloging-in-Publication Data
Puckett, Margaret B.
  Understanding infant development / Margaret B. Puckett and Janet K. Black with Joseph M. Moriarity. -- 1st ed.
        p. cm.
    Includes bibliographical references and index.
    ISBN 978-1-933653-01-3
    1. Infants--Development.   I. Black, Janet K. II. Moriarity, Joseph M. III. Title.
    HQ774.P83 2006
    305.231--dc22
                                    2006034662

Printed on acid-free paper.

Understanding Infant Development

Introduction

Whether you are a parent or an early childhood professional, you know that caring for and raising children are rewarding challenges: They represent the best of times and the worst of times—sometimes at virtually the same time!

Raising children in the United States has become even more difficult over the past few decades. Parents work more hours, commute farther, are more stressed, and have less free time than ever before. The media and our consumer culture do not always act in the best interest of our children. Ads targeted directly at even very young children constantly promote unhealthy foods, as do many TV shows, movies, toys, and games. Much of the entertainment that popular media offers is violent, even those shows supposedly designed for children, and more than a thousand studies have shown that movie and television violence fosters real violence.

At the same time, parents and other caregivers now have more accurate information available to them about how children develop and how adults can support their growth and development. This knowledge is critical for those who are responsible for the care and education of young children.

This book is designed to give you a comprehensive overview of the most relevant theories and research on infant development. You will learn much about current knowledge in a number of areas, including:

- the impact and long-term effects of biology and environment on early brain development

- the influence of culture on growth and development
- how children learn
- important theories of child development
- how early life experiences lay the groundwork for language acquisition and thinking
- the effects of nurturing care on emotional development and stability later in life

You'll also discover that research has challenged many traditional theories on how best to support infant growth and development. At the same time, some of the old tried-and-true theories are still relevant today. What is important in the end is that the child development theories and current research presented here help parents and early childhood professionals improve the quality of life and education for children in their care.

This book also introduces you to two fictional children, Jeremy and Angela, whose ongoing development is tracked throughout this and the other two books in this series in order to help illustrate various behaviors and stages of development. Their family background and birth details are listed below.

THE STORY OF TWO FAMILIES

Both in their early thirties, Ann and Bill decided they wanted to have a child a few years after they married. As soon as Ann became pregnant, the two began attending childbirth classes and reading books about child care and development. Their son, Jeremy, was born full-term.

Cheryl is fifteen years old and lives with her mother and four brothers and sisters. She had been seeing her boyfriend, James, for about seven months when she found out she was pregnant. Cheryl had no prenatal care until she was six months pregnant. Her child, Angela, was born prematurely.

Part One

Physical and Motor Development

Infancy conforms to nobody—all conform to it.

—RALPH WALDO EMERSON

In part 1, we'll explore the remarkable physical and motor growth that takes place in infants during their first year, and we'll examine the key theories of physical and motor development. We will also examine how much of this growth is based on inheritance and how much is a product of the family and the culture into which an infant is born. You'll learn about early brain growth and neurological development, as well as the importance of taking advantage of *windows of opportunity* in supporting infants and young children's development.

Definition: *Windows of opportunity*—special times during growth and development when vital connections in the brain can be strengthened if infants and young children have certain kinds of experiences.

The physical and motor abilities that develop during the first year help expand the infant's emotional and social world. By becoming more familiar with the factors that affect infants' physical and motor development, you'll be better able to create an environment that encourages and supports that growth, and you'll be more likely to notice if a child's development begins to fall behind that of other children of similar age. You'll see how motor experiences in infancy—touching, rolling, reaching, and so on—are essential factors in a child's *cognitive development*.

Definition: *Cognitive development*—the part of development that deals with thinking, problem solving, intelligence, and language.

Given that each day 13 million children spend part or all of their day in nonparental care, early childhood professionals play a crucial role in supporting physical and motor development in infants.

What researchers have learned by looking closely at how different children grow and develop in different environments, families, and cultures can contribute to your understanding of the needs of the children in your care. This knowledge can help you recognize the ways your interactions with them can affect their physical and motor growth, and it can also help you understand what you can—and cannot—expect of them at different ages.

1

Theories of Physical and Motor Development

When a child is born, parents, friends, and relatives almost immediately start trying to guess what kind of person this newborn will be. Does she look more like her dad or her mom? Will he be quiet or a ball of energy? Will she be fussy and demanding or calm and easygoing? We can all agree that some qualities, like eye and skin color, are inherited from our parents. And most people also agree that how and where we grow up also affect the kind of person we become.

But where is the dividing line? How much of our personality is inherited (nature) and how much is affected by how we are raised (nurture)? This question of nature versus nurture has puzzled people for a long time. During the last one hundred years, a number of theories have emerged about how growth happens, why it follows certain paths, what causes us to behave in certain ways, and how and why we have some abilities and talents but not others.

Some researchers and child psychologists think that growth and development are controlled mainly by heredity—that we are born with a kind of blueprint that defines when and how much each aspect of growth and development will happen. These scientists say that as we get older, how we develop physically, emotionally, and psychologically is entirely a function of traits that were part of us—in our genes—when we were born. Over time, they simply emerge like a chicken hatching from an egg.

This is called the *maturationist* theory.

Other researchers and theorists believe that the environment in which we grow up plays a much more important role in our development and growth. According to this theory, called *behaviorism*, our family life and culture—how we're rewarded and punished for how we behave and learn, what educational opportunities we have, what our significant authority and peer relationships are like, and so on—affect and shape the kind of adult we become much more than our genes.

Advocates of another theory, *developmental interaction*, take a different view. They say children are born with certain abilities that can develop and blossom when they are supported by a rich and stimulating environment. This theory also holds that having little stimulation and few rewards and mental challenges will retard growth and learning.

Still other theorists and educators suggest a *transactional perspective*, in which a person's inherited traits and environmental experiences affect each other through regular interactions between heredity and environment. In other words, inherited traits are shaped by experience *and* experience is shaped by inherited traits. They say that interaction between nature and nurture happens not just while we are infants but throughout our life. This perspective has been important in the study of human growth and development because it suggests that as development happens, new characteristics or traits that were not present in the original fertilized egg develop as a result of the interaction between heredity and environment. For example, a child who is shy from birth may grow up in a home where the parents are sensitive and supportive, and they may help the child trust and relate more easily to others. Slowly, over time, this child can become more comfortable meeting and getting to know new people. He may overcome his shyness.

Perhaps the most prominent theory of child growth, development, and learning today, the *systems approach* proposes that a variety of influences affect who we become. These influences include biology, race, cultural and religious values, family and ethnic traditions, gender, financial status, and more. For example, different families and cultural groups have different ideas about when crawling and walking should begin and how parents and other caregivers should encourage these skills. Some families or groups keep infants tightly wrapped during their early months, or limit where infants can explore by placing them in a playpen or in one room. Others encourage early walking by providing infants with greater freedom of movement. Children may be given free use of the environment to encourage motor skills as they roll over, crawl, pull up, walk, and use special toys and equipment. This last example is more common in Western cultures, in which all sorts of products, such as floor mats, baby swings, pull and push toys, and climbing toys are popular with parents and caregivers.

It's now commonly accepted that humans are genetically programmed for coordination, movement, and mobility. Environmental differences during early childhood can mean, however, that different children will begin developing different motor abilities (holding things, crawling, walking) at different ages. Such differences in when infants begin to learn particular skills are viewed as simply that—different, neither good nor bad, neither normal nor abnormal. This perspective encourages us to acknowledge and appreciate each child's uniqueness and individuality.

Creating a Way to Understand Children's Growth, Development, and Learning

You certainly don't need to know all these developmental theories in great detail to be an effective early childhood professional. When we interact with children, whether as parents, child care professionals, teachers, or just friends, parts of all these theories can apply and help us define some basic principles of growth and development to guide our thinking.

Growth and development depend on the interaction between children's heredity, the place and culture in which they grow up, and the experiences they have.

The following principles are generally accepted as true for all children, regardless of their race and culture.

1. The interaction between a child's heredity and the experiences she has with her family and within her environment and culture shapes her growth and development.
2. A child's physical growth and development generally moves from the head downward and from the center of the body outward. For example, during infancy and early childhood, the muscles of the upper body become more mature and coordinated than those of the lower parts of the body, with the large muscles of the hips and upper legs developing before the smaller muscles of the lower legs, ankles, and feet. Tremendous brain growth and development happen before birth and through the first three years of life.
3. Most children follow similar development patterns, and one stage (e.g., crawling) prepares the way for the next (e.g., walking), just as babbling sounds come before word formation.
4. There are certain times when children are much more sensitive to the effects of the world around them. Many studies show that during these *windows of opportunity* certain expe-

riences have the greatest positive—or negative—effects on physical and mental growth.

5. While the patterns for growth and development are similar among children, the speed at which any one child reaches *developmental milestones* (important stages in physical and mental growth, such as learning to crawl, walk, talk, and read) can vary. One child may begin walking without help at nine months, while another may begin at fifteen months. There are great differences in the rate at which children learn to read too. For example, one child may begin reading at age four, while another still struggles to read at age seven, but by the time they are teenagers, they both may read equally well.

6. Children do not mature emotionally, physically, and mentally at the same time or at the same rate. For instance, a child's intellectual development may be ahead of his or her emotional or social development. Another child may be very coordinated but have somewhat poor language skills.

Over the course of their lives, children's growth, development, learning, and behaviors are also affected by cultural and societal factors, including access to nutritious food, health care practices, family goals and values, access to education, the education level of family members, economic level, the political situation of their community and nation, and many more.

Social and Cultural Influences on Development

Despite physical and genetic differences, most infants eventually reach the developmental milestones and goals needed to survive and take part in their own cultures. The many cultures on our planet each have their own view about how children should be cared for and what they should be taught. Here are a few examples of ways in which cultures around the world vary in child development beliefs and practices.

THE BIRTHING PROCESS

Birthing procedures around the world range widely. In some cultures, mothers receive limited or no help during birthing, not even from family and friends. In other cultures, midwives or family members help with the birth, and in still others, babies are born in very high-tech hospitals with professional health care staff who have had special training. In some developing countries, women still give birth in quite primitive conditions. Most industrialized nations treat birth as a medical procedure that takes place in the controlled conditions of a hospital and is overseen by medical professionals. In many countries, including Western countries such as the Netherlands, England, and Sweden, many women still choose to have their babies at home, with the assistance of a midwife and family members.

CARRYING, CUDDLING, AND TRANSPORTING THE INFANT

In some tribal and rural cultures in Africa, Asia, and South America, infants are carried all day long, tied on their mothers' backs or carried in a sling or pouch at their mothers' sides while the mothers go about their daily chores. Infant and mother are rarely separated, and the infant may be breast-fed on demand throughout the day. Some babies are carried this way until the age of two, three, or even four.

In contrast, in Western cultures, babies are generally carried upright, peering over the shoulder of their parent or caregiver, or they are transported in a variety of devices, including strollers, carriages, car seats, and other carriers.

INFANT CRYING

In some cultures, infants' cries are seen as a warning signal. Parents and other caregivers respond quickly with food, patting, or holding. In other cultures, such as in the United States, adults often wait a bit before responding, as they try to decide how upset the baby is and whether he will become quiet without help.

SLEEPING WITH INFANTS

In cultures where extended families are still more intact and family members depend on each other more for support and identity (such as in Asia, Africa, and Latin America), children commonly sleep with one or both parents or siblings for some years. Many young children around the world sleep in the same room with their parents even when other rooms are available. In many homes in the United States and other Western industrialized countries, where independence is more of a value and space is less of an issue, infants and especially young children are much less likely to sleep with their parents.

NONPARENTAL CHILD CARE

Cultures also differ in their ideas about who should take care of children. Before the 1960s, North Americans and many Europeans, like many cultures rooted in traditional, pre–twentieth-century patriarchal cultures around the world, believed that mothers should not work outside of the home, but should stay at home and raise their children. In an increasing number of countries today, however, particularly in industrialized and technologically advanced countries like the United States, Europe, and parts of Asia, mothers from a variety of cultural backgrounds either choose to work or are forced to work out of financial need and must rely on others for child care.

In some Native American tribes, like many other tribal and traditional cultures around the world, all members of the family and immediate community are expected to help raise a child, whether or not the child's mother is around. Grandmothers, aunts, male relatives, and older siblings frequently share responsibility for infants. This is one of the main reasons why even in the United States, Latin American, Somali, and other immigrant families from traditional cultures with extended families still intact are less likely to put their children in preschool or child care.

Through these examples, you can see how widely people's views can differ about how to raise children. And yet, adults all over the world have a similar goal: to help their young develop the abilities they'll need to survive and thrive in their cultures as adults. Given the wide differences in child-rearing and education practices among cultures, we still need to try to answer these basic questions for all children: "What are the common goals of child growth and development?" and "What are the skills that are essential not only to survive, but to have satisfying, constructive, and productive lives?" Thinking about these questions can help you look at and understand your own beliefs. Knowing how much culture affects a child's development and learning can also help you appreciate the many roads children travel on their way to becoming adults.

Today, we can identify four important and basic goals for growing children:

- learning to control their emotions, behaviors, and attention
- developing language and the ability to think and solve problems
- learning to relate to others and to form and keep friendships
- achieving and maintaining healthy bodies and taking on more and more responsibility for their own health and safety

In this chapter, we discussed the major theories of physical and motor development, as well as the cultural attitudes and practices that can affect that development. Next, we'll turn our attention to early brain growth and development, the many changes infants must make once they leave their mothers' wombs, and the unconscious reflexes they have that help them survive in the "outside" world.

2 Early Brain Growth and Neurological Development

Newborns enter the world with remarkable abilities. To go from the womb to the world outside of it, a newborn must go through a number of dramatic physical changes. First, she must begin breathing immediately. She must also begin to eat and eliminate body wastes. For nine months, she lived in a soft, quiet place surrounded by the warm fluid of her mother's womb and comforted by the sound of her mother's heartbeat. Suddenly, the newborn is surrounded by cool, dry air and a bright, noisy, and busy world. For the first time, she has many new sensory experiences: sight, sound, smell, touch, taste, and *kinesthesis*. Despite these changes, most infants come into our world able to survive easily.

Definition: *Kinesthesis*—being aware of one's body, its position, and its movement.

The spinal column, the brain, and an amazing network of nerve cells, or *neurons*, make up the newborn's nervous system—this is where *neurological development* takes place. The nervous system has three interconnected functions (Delcomyn 1998):

- to receive and interpret information about what's happening inside and outside of the body

- to make decisions about this information
- to organize and carry out actions based on this information

We humans have very sophisticated ways of receiving and understanding information through our *sensory system*, which includes all of the sense organs of the body and sensory neurons. These neurons, or nerve cells, carry information from the sense organs to other parts of the nervous system. The *motor system* includes the muscles, certain glands, and the motor nerves, which make our muscles and glands work.

There is a third system—called the *integrating system*—that takes information from the sensory system, looks at the memory of past experiences, and then makes decisions based on both the old and the new information. It's called the integrating system because it brings together many sources of information from many different parts of the nervous system.

In the introduction to part 1, we briefly introduced the phrase *windows of opportunity*, a very important concept for anyone who cares for children. Windows of opportunity are special times during the growth and development of infants and young children when vital connections in their brains can be strengthened if they have certain kinds of experiences. Many windows of opportunity occur during the first three years of a child's life, particularly for brain development associated with emotional connections to others (called *attachment*), emotional control, the ability to cope with stress, vision, and motor development.

Table 2.1: Windows of Opportunity in Early Brain Growth and Neurological Development

Age	Developmental Area
Birth to 2 years	Social attachment, ability to cope with stress
Birth to 3 years	Emotional control
Birth to 2 years	Ability to see and hear
Birth to 3 years	Vocabulary
Birth to 5 years	Motor development and coordination
Birth to 10 years	First- and second-language development
1 to 5 years	Mathematical and logical thinking
3 to 10 years	Music appreciation and learning

The idea of windows of opportunity is often misunderstood to mean that after a particular age, the opportunity for specific types of brain development or learning is lost if certain types of experiences have not occurred (the window closes, so to speak). While there are prime times for specific types of brain growth, new research is showing that our brains are far more flexible than we once thought. In fact, various types of growth and development can take place throughout our life span. Missing some windows of opportunity, in general, can have a smaller effect if a child has appropriately challenging, nurturing, and enriching experiences as he grows up. For example, children who have never been read to at home, or who have seen few reading materials before entering school, can still learn to read well. They will likely learn more slowly, however, than children who have had previous experience with books and reading.

Reflexes

Healthy, full-term babies are born prepared for life outside the womb. They have a number of inborn movement patterns, called *reflexes*, that help them adjust to new surroundings and new demands. For the most part, these early reflexes—for example, the grasping and startle reflexes—are a function of brain-stem and spinal-cord mechanisms rather than a function of the "thinking" part of the brain, the *cerebral cortex*, which gives us our senses, memory, and thoughts. Some reflexes are called *survival reflexes* because they are necessary for the infant to stay alive. Breathing is an obvious example.

Definitions: *Reflexes*—built-in (not learned) automatic responses to stimuli, resulting from earliest brain and muscle development.

Survival reflexes—reflexes essential to sustaining life (such as breathing) or protecting our bodies (such as closing our eyes when an object comes toward them).

Table 2.2: **Major Reflexes Present in Infancy**

Reflex	Description
SURVIVAL REFLEXES	
Breathing reflex	Infant inhales and exhales, giving oxygen to the red blood cells and removing carbon dioxide.
Rooting reflex	Infant turns in the direction of a touch on the cheek as though searching for a nipple; serves to orient the infant to the breast or the bottle.
Sucking and swallowing reflex	Infant is stimulated by a nipple placed in the mouth; this allows the infant to take in nourishment.
Eye blink and pupillary reflex	Infant's eyes close or blink; pupils dilate or constrict to protect the eyes.
PRIMITIVE REFLEXES	
Grasping reflex	Infant holds firmly to an object touching the palm of the hand. Its disappearance around the fourth month is a sign of growing brain development.
Moro reflex	Often called the startle reflex; a loud noise or sudden jolt will cause the infant's arms to push outward, then return to an embrace-like position. It disappears around the fifth or sixth month.
Babinski reflex	Infant's toes fan outward, then curl when the bottom of the foot is stroked. It disappears by the end of the first year.
Tonic neck reflex	A "fencing pose" often assumed when sleeping; infant's head turns to one side, arm extends on the same side, and opposite arm and leg flex at the elbow and knee. It disappears around seven months.

Jeremy, at forty-eight hours old, is in his mother's arms, sleeping quite soundly. His face is scrunched into a tight expression: eyes tightly closed, mouth shut, chin almost buried in his chest. He is wrapped in a soft baby blanket, with his arms folded comfortably against his chest, his knees bent slightly upward, and his toes pointed inward.

His mother, Ann, tries to wake him by gently rubbing her fingers across his soft cheek. He squirms slightly, stretching his legs and turning his head toward the touch; his mouth opens slightly, but he falls back to sleep. His mouth makes faint sucking movements briefly before he drifts into a fairly deep sleep.

Home from the neonatal care unit, Angela, at two weeks old, is crying loudly. Her legs stretch stiffly and her arms and hands wave in the air. Her blanket is twisted, and her mother is in a hurry to fix a bottle to feed her. As the nipple of the bottle brushes against her lips, Angela searches and tries to grasp it. Her sucking response is somewhat weak, and she whimpers until she succeeds in getting the nipple and her hunger pains begin to go away. The warmth and comfort of food calm her.

Reference

Delcomyn, F. 1998. *Foundations of neurobiology.* New York: Freeman.

3 Physical and Motor Development

The rate and complexity of infants' growth and development during the first year of life are remarkable. In fact, in no other one-year period until puberty do so many physical changes happen! The changes during infancy are so rapid that we measure them in days and weeks rather than months and years (Anselmo 1987).

Physical Characteristics

Newborns often lose weight in the first few days after birth because they lose body fluids and aren't able to eat well. But they then gain weight at a rate of six to eight ounces per week. In the first five to six months, they can as much as double their birth weight, and their length will increase by six to seven inches. During the second half of the first year, growth slows somewhat, though it still continues at a rapid pace. If human growth were to continue at this pace, an eighteen-year-old would be more than fifteen feet tall and weigh several tons! Fortunately, growth slows down quite a bit after the first two years.

Changes in weight and height are easy to see. But much internal growth is taking place too. Infants' central nervous systems mature, their bones and muscles grow in weight and length, and their overall coordination increases. The soft bones of early infancy gradually harden. The bones of the skull and wrists harden first, and the wrists and ankles develop more bones as the child gets older. Although infants are born with all the muscle cells they will ever have, there is a large amount of water in that muscle tissue. Gradually, protein and other nutrients replace this fluid, and infants' muscle strength increases.

Expected Patterns and Developmental Milestones

The timing and order of development can vary among and within cultures and racial groups. As mentioned earlier, geographic, cultural, social, and economic factors can either help or hinder growth and development. Parental involvement also affects growth and development through the quality and timing of nurture, play, and discipline. This can be enriching in many ways: educational, emotional, and psychological. As you look at the following table, remember that these patterns are based on averages; there will always be differences among children.

As a child care professional, it's important for you to be aware of these developmental milestones and to pay close attention to the children in your care so that you will notice when a child's development begins to fall behind other children of similar age.

Table 3.1: **Developmental Milestones in Motor Control during the First Year**

Age	Motor Development
Birth to 3 months	Supports head when in prone position
	Lifts head
	Supports weight on elbows
	Hands relax from the grasping reflex
	Visually follows a moving object
	Pushes with feet against lap when held upright
	Makes reflexive stepping movements when held in a standing position
	Sits with support
	Turns from side to back
3 to 6 months	Slaps at bathwater
	Kicks feet when prone
	Plays with toes

	Reaches for but misses a hanging object
	Shakes and stares at toy placed in hand
	Holds head up when held at shoulder
	Turns from back to side
	Sits with props
	Makes effort to sit alone
	Displays crawling behaviors
	Rocks on all fours
	Draws knees up and falls forward
6 to 9 months	Rolls from back to stomach
	Crawls using both hands and feet
	Sits alone steadily
	Pulls up to standing position in crib
	Raises self to sitting posture
	Successfully reaches and holds toys
	Transfers object from one hand to the other
	Stands up with help from furniture
	Moves along crib rail
	Makes stepping movements around furniture
9 to 12 months	Practices "mature" crawling
	Moves while holding on to furniture
	Walks with two hands held
	Sits without falling
	Stands alone
	May walk alone
	Attempts to crawl up stairs
	Grasps object with thumb and forefinger

The Connection between Physical and Motor Development and Perception

As noted earlier, in infancy, motor experiences—which include touching, rolling, and reaching—are primary factors in the growth of the child's thinking ability. At first, movements are unintentional (as with many reflexes) but soon, most have purpose. This stage of development follows a pattern from random, reflex activity to planned and intended behavior. In other words, as infants become more aware of the world around them, they truly *want* to explore it.

We now know, too, that an environment rich in sights, sounds, tastes, smells, textures, and movements fosters brain growth and development, especially when combined with touching, talking, singing, sharing books, and other forms of positive interaction.

PERCEPTUAL-MOTOR DEVELOPMENT

Perception is the process of using our senses to take in information about the world around us. It involves all of our senses. For instance, sight, or visual perception, gives us the ability to recognize and see the differences between faces, patterns, sizes, shapes, depth, distance, and so on. Hearing, or auditory perception, also gives us information that helps us identify people, objects, and events, and together with sight helps us make sense of such qualities as distance, speed, and space. Our ability to feel things gives us important information relating to touch, textures, temperature, weight, pressure, and our own body position and movement. Our senses of smell and taste give us additional information—and pleasure too.

Perceptual-motor development refers to the relationship between a child's perceptions and his motor responses. A child's motor abilities can influence perceptual development and, likewise, perception can have a strong effect on a child's motor-skill development. The development of an infant's perception of space, depth, and weight, for example, greatly depends on her locomotor experiences. Similarly, a child's motor development greatly depends on her ability to perceive her environment. For a child to successfully reach for a toy and pick it up, he must integrate visual information about where that toy is in relation to his arm.

Relationship of Physical and Motor Development to Psychosocial Development

Growing physical and motor abilities during the first year also help expand the infant's emotional and social world. By communicating hunger, pain, and happiness through crying, cooing, and other noises, infants learn that they can get others to interact with them. When these interactions are positive and helpful, infants learn to trust parents and caregivers—and *themselves*—to meet their needs.

Each new developmental milestone brings with it new sets of behaviors and new types of interactions between infants and caregivers. Ideally, each new ability brings encouragement, praise, and joy from caregivers, which strengthens the child's self-confidence and his emerging sense of identity.

As motor abilities increase, parents, siblings, and caregivers often begin to see the infant as more "grown up." As a result, they might also think the infant is more capable than she really is. They may, for example, expect the infant to hold her own bottle for feeding or manage playthings designed for older children. Such misjudgment can cause unsafe situations and harm the infant's growing but fragile sense of confidence.

As infants are more able to get around by themselves, safety becomes a real and immediate concern, and caregivers need to learn to communicate with infants in new ways, including the use of facial expression and vocal tone. Keeping children safe while encouraging exploration activities that develop their muscles and coordination requires both care and understanding.

Too many commands and limits from caregivers, particularly if said with impatience and anger, frighten and confuse infants. Such commands can also damage a child's self-confidence and hinder her willingness to explore, learn, and express herself. While there are times caregivers need to say "no" and "don't touch," doing this too often can cause an infant to have negative feelings about the people who mean the most to him. It's much better for parents and other caregivers to create safe, child-friendly environments where the child won't have to hear "no" or "be careful" too often.

> *Ideally, each new ability brings encouragement, praise, and joy from caregivers, which strengthens the child's self-confidence and his emerging sense of identity.*

The next chapter looks more closely at the impact of psychological, emotional, and social factors on an infant's physical, neurological, and motor development, including those factors that child care professionals can most influence.

Reference

Anselmo, S. 1987. *Early childhood development: Prenatal through age eight.* Columbus, Ohio: Merrill.

4 Factors Influencing Physical and Motor Development

An interplay of many genetic, psychological, sociological, and environmental factors affect the quality and progression of an infant's physical and motor development.

Genetic Makeup

Each infant is a unique individual with a special genetic makeup. Some examples of genetic traits are obvious: physical features such as eye, hair, and skin color; shape and size of facial features; body build; and so on. Genes also affect mental, psychological, and social characteristics. Examples include temperament and the likelihood of having certain skills and talents, such as math or music, as well as certain psychological traits and disorders.

Prenatal Development

During the nine months in the mother's womb, the growth of the fetus is very rapid. It's very important during this time for the mother to protect the fetus from hazards such as drugs (including nicotine, alcohol, and both prescription and street drugs) and environmental toxins. Immediate and long-term damage can happen to the fetus as a result of exposure to such hazards. Infants whose life in the womb is free of drugs, toxins, unhealthy foods, maternal stress, and other hazards are less likely to experience problems later with their health, growth, and development.

Socioeconomic Status

Infant and family well-being depend on having adequate food, shelter, clothing, transportation, and access to health care. How well these family needs are met usually depends on income and available resources both in the family and in the community.

Families may need and be eligible for local, state, and federal assistance. Programs such as the U.S. Special Supplemental Nutrition Program for Women, Infants, and Children (WIC) and the State Children's Health Insurance Program (SCHIP) can contribute to infant and family well-being. Too often, however, families who most need these programs do not know about them or do not know how to participate in them.

Poverty has both immediate and long-term effects on child growth, development, and learning. Children living in poverty are more likely not to have enough to eat or to have nutritious food. They may have little or no access to health care, including needed childhood immunizations, dental care, and timely treatment for illnesses, infections, and injuries. Parents who are stressed by money problems may have little time or energy to give their children adequate nurturing, playful interactions, and good learning opportunities. Families receiving welfare assistance or in which parents are starting a new job or work training often find that the cost of child care for infants is too expensive. They may then be forced to make arrangements that do not provide the best nurturing and learning for the child.

Opportunities to Interact, Explore, and Play

Each new skill increases an infant's ability to interact with people and the world around her. Infants like to look at colorful objects. They enjoy listening to our voices and to recordings of pleasing or familiar sounds and music. They enjoy it when parents or caregivers talk, laugh, imitate their actions, play peek-a-boo and pat-a-cake, and help them explore. Playing with other infants and their caregivers is the "job" of an infant. It is the key to all parts of their growth and development.

Safety

At this age, the combination of an infant's ability to explore on his own, his great curiosity about the world around him, and the fact that he has not been in the world long enough to develop common sense means that safety must be a main concern for all caregivers. The most common safety concerns during a child's first year are automobile accidents, falls, burns, choking or suffocation, poisoning, and drowning. Adults' failure to recognize infants' changing abilities and curiosity is often the reason infants are injured.

AN INFANT'S SPACES AND FURNISHINGS

The infant's surroundings must be clean and examined regularly for potential dangers: objects on the floor that could scratch, cut, or go into the mouth (such as balloons, coins, marbles, small toy parts, buttons, and safety pins); exposed electrical outlets and electrical wires that could be pulled or mouthed; furnishings—for example, shelves and changing tables, that fall easily; toxic substances within easy reach (such as medicines, cosmetics, household cleaning and gardening supplies, and arts and crafts products); poisonous plants; hot water faucets and unsanitary toilet bowls; and many others.

All baby equipment and clothing should meet current safety standards. These standards apply to cribs, car seats, swings, playpens, walkers, pacifiers, toys, and all other baby supplies and equipment. The Consumer Product Safety Commission regularly publishes information about safe products for children and items that have been recalled because they are hazardous. Caregivers can get this information online at no cost.

SELECTING TOYS

Toys should be chosen carefully. Age-appropriate toys are made of pieces that are too large to swallow, are lightweight and easily held, and have no sharp edges, batteries, or small removable parts. They are made of washable, nontoxic materials and are strong enough to survive children's play.

SUDDEN INFANT DEATH SYNDROME (SIDS)

SIDS is the sudden and unexpected death of an apparently healthy infant during the first year. It is the most common cause of death between one and six months of age, and it most often happens between two and four months of age. In the past, scientists thought that infants who died in their cribs had smothered in their covers (thus the term *crib death*). Since the 1960s, much research has been done on SIDS, but its actual cause or causes are still unclear.

SIDS seems to have decreased in recent years, thanks in part to a Back to Sleep campaign. The Back to Sleep campaign has tried to educate parents and other caregivers about SIDS and the importance of placing infants on their backs. This practice is now common, and researchers believe that the apparent drop in SIDS deaths is due to this change.

Abuse and Neglect

There are generally three types of abuse: physical, emotional or psychological (most often caused when a child is cursed at, belittled, ignored, or rejected), and sexual. Infants and children under age three are particularly susceptible to child abuse. Frustration over the infant crying (due to colic and other discomforts), changing hundreds of diapers, the demands of feeding schedules and finicky appetites, a lack of sleep, and other stresses may lead an adult to abuse an infant. Postpartum depression in the mother, family stress (marital, economic, psychological, etc.), and lack of knowledge about child development are factors often harder to confirm and address.

A common form of physical abuse known as *shaken baby syndrome* happens mostly to infants younger than six months of age. Shaking an infant or small child can cause serious physical and mental damage or even death.

Failure to Thrive

Some children who are raised in very poor or neglectful conditions during the first year of life show signs of severe developmental delays. These infants have slower physical growth and skeletal development, and their heights and weights are far below what is common for their ages. Neglected children are more likely to become sick, have more stomach upsets, and be emotionally fragile.

Neglect can take different forms, including poor nutrition and lack of proper clothing, shelter, supervision, and protection. Sometimes neglect includes denial of medical attention. Intellectual stimulation and emotional support may also be missing. Some infants are simply abandoned.

Some children raised in very poor or neglectful conditions during the first year of life show signs of severe developmental delays.

Abuse and neglect can occur in any family, regardless of income level, ethnic group, or family configuration (one-parent, two-parent, extended, large, and small families). All states have child abuse reporting laws under which suspected child abuse *must* be reported to appropriate authorities.

Infants with Special Needs

Infants whose prenatal development was less than perfect due to poverty, the mother's health complications, poor nutrition, premature birth, or some other birth trauma are often identified as being *at risk*. This means that their growth and development will likely be complicated by conditions that require specialized care, treatment, and educational practices. Infants who are at risk for poor or delayed development or who have disabling conditions need assessment and identification so that they can receive any special care they need.

In addition to getting help as soon as possible, infants with special needs require knowledge and special sensitivity from their caregivers. Sometimes, the challenges of caring for an infant with special needs can be very difficult for parents, family members, and other caregivers. Today, statewide systems offer early intervention services. The law provides for the following groups of children:

- infants and children who have a measurable delay in their physical, motor, social, emotional, and/or cognitive development, especially those who have a difficult time adapting to their environments and achieving autonomy
- children who have a physical or mental condition that could result in a developmental delay (such as Down syndrome, multiple sclerosis, sensory impairments, cerebral palsy, or autism)
- children who are at risk of experiencing a developmental delay, as determined by the state, if intervention is not provided

Table 4.1: When to Worry about At-Risk Infants and Toddlers (Andrew 1998)

Age	Phase	Primary Tasks	Warning Signs
0 to 3 months	Taking in	Crying for basic needs, developing attention, calming when needs met	Poor head control, no social smile, no visual/auditory responses, feeding problems, difficult to soothe, not attentive to faces
4 to 8 months	Reaching out	Attachment to adult, expanding interest in toys and people	No sitting, no mobility, no vocalizations, not seeking attention, not interested in toys/objects, feeding and sleeping problems
9 to 14 months	Moving out	Exploration, communication	Not moving from one position to another, asymmetric movement, no imitation, rigid play routines, no gestural or verbal communication

14 to 20 months	Speaking up	Learning by imitation, seeking independence	Not walking, not talking, not understanding directions, not using objects for intended purposes
21 to 30 months	Speaking out	Imagination, communication	Few words, no word combinations, no constructive or imaginative play, persistent withdrawn or aggressive behaviors
30 to 42 months	Playing along	Independence, peer relations	Does not attend to age-appropriate tasks to completion, withdrawn or repetitive behaviors that cannot be interrupted, unintelligible speech, tantrums, lack of independence in self-help skills

Reference

Andrew, C. 1998. "When to worry about infants and toddlers 'at risk.'" *Focus on Infants and Toddlers* 11:2. Copyright © 1998 by the Association for Childhood Education International (ACEI). Reprinted with permission from the Association for Childhood Education International, 17904 Georgia Avenue, Suite 215, Onley, MD.

The Role of the Early Childhood Professional

1. Always keep an eye out for infants who might have special needs and require timely assessment and help.

2. Be sure infants are able to interact regularly with staff and other children, have toys that interest them, and have the chance to explore their world.

3. Create an environment where each infant feels loved and cared for each day.

4. Create an environment where infants feel physically and emotionally safe as they start to explore the world around them more and more.

5. Get to know the parents of your infants and help them in whatever ways you can.

6. Know all the current health and safety alerts, regulations, and laws that protect infants and young children and follow them rigorously in your setting.

7. Get to know resources in the community that could help you and the infants' parents.

Discussion Questions

1. How would you describe your own developmental theory in relation to the theories mentioned in chapter 1, with their emphasis on nature and nurture? Name some specific examples of how your personal theory influences how you interact with the infants in your care (e.g., through programming, behavior intervention, communication style, etc.).

2. What aspects of your child care practice do you feel are influenced by your sociocultural background? Do the children in your care share your background? What modifications might you make in your caregiving practices to be more inclusive of different backgrounds?

3. List some developmental milestones you've recently observed in the infants in your care. Based on what you've now read about infant development, if one infant is developmentally lagging behind another, what might be the cause and what are your options for addressing this delay? At what point should you be concerned that an infant in your care merits assessment by a professional?

4. Based on your reading of the recommended practices in chapter 4 regarding age-appropriate interactions, safety, furnishings, and toys, can you identify any areas where you could make improvements in your practice or setting? Make a list of potential improvements and a plan for resolving them.

Further Reading

Cryer, D., and T. Harms, eds. 2000. *Infants and toddlers in out-of-home care.* Baltimore: P. Brookes.

Gandini, L., and C. P. Edwards, eds. 2000. *Bambini: The Italian approach to infant/toddler care.* New York: Teachers College Press.

National Child Care Information Center (NCCIC). http://nccic.org

Rogoff, B. 2003. *The cultural nature of human development.* New York: Oxford University Press.

Shelov, S. P., ed. 1998. *Your baby's first year.* New York: Bantam Books.

Part Two

Psychosocial Development

The first cry of a newborn baby in Chicago or Zamboango, in Amsterdam or Rangoon, has the same pitch and key, each saying, "I am! I have come through! I belong! I am a member of the Family!"

—CARL SANDBURG

An infant's social and emotional development is less easy to interpret and measure than the more obvious physical characteristics and motor skills of infancy and early childhood. Infants' ways of expressing emotions and needs—and of showing that they want to interact with others—are, of course, initially quite primitive. At first, infants are limited to crying and using body language to communicate. Within the first twelve months, however, their communication skills begin to improve dramatically. They begin to understand how their caregivers relate to them. They begin to trust their own ability to get attention and to control their emotions. And many even begin to use language.

Also, infants' caregivers get better at understanding the meanings of the noises, cries, and gestures infants make. Emotional and social development during infancy depends on the ability of caregivers to understand and respond appropriately to infants' expressions of emotion and to their desire for social interaction.

In part 2, you'll learn to recognize and understand the important theories associated with psychological and social (psychosocial) development—the development of infants' minds and how they interact with others. This knowledge can help in important ways: it can help you better understand the abilities and needs of the infants in your care, and it can help you form expectations that are appropriate to an infant's specific age and maturity level. You'll understand more about the important effects of early psychosocial experiences on brain growth and early neurological development.

You'll also see how important essential experiences are to infants' psychosocial development during the first year and you'll discover ways to provide those experiences and supplement them. You'll become familiar with major social and emotional milestones in infancy and you'll be able to recognize and shape factors that influence infants' psychosocial development. In short, you'll better understand the role caregivers like you can play in fostering healthy psychosocial development in infants.

5 Theories of Psychosocial Development

The study of psychology in general, and emotional and social development in particular, helps us better understand how humans behave and what unseen mental processes affect and guide our individual behaviors. A number of theories have been developed over the years to explain emotional and social development. We will discuss four of the most influential theories, each of which has made a unique contribution to our current understanding of infants' emotional and social development during their first months of life. We'll touch briefly on two of these theories—the *psychoanalytic theory* of the early pioneer Sigmund Freud and Albert Bandura's *social learning theory*—but we will spend most of this chapter reviewing Erik Erikson's *eight stages of psychosocial development* and John Bowlby and Mary Ainsworth's *attachment theory*, both of which have had a significant influence on how parents and other caretakers nurture and educate young children today.

Freud's Psychoanalytic Psychology

Sigmund Freud (1856–1939) was the first psychoanalyst to suggest a theory of personality based on underlying psychological foundations and needs. For example, Freud believed that behaviors were controlled by unconscious desires and hidden motives. He was among the first to suggest that personality development continues through a series of stages during which certain conflicts must be successfully solved before the individual moves ahead to the next stage. He believed that solving these stage-related conflicts would, over time, result in healthy development.

Freud created the idea of *fixation*, which says that certain psychological behaviors might not move beyond a particular point in development. As a result, a person would carry an immature behavior or way of solving problems into later life. This would result in unhealthy psychological growth. Freud believed that early experiences determined the path and characteristics of later development and behavior. Further, he suggested that individuals are born with *psychosexual* instincts that change over the years from infancy to maturity.

While many of his specific theories are called into question by modern researchers and early childhood professionals, Freud laid the foundation for the pioneers in child development research.

Definition: *Psychosexual*—the mental, emotional, and behavioral aspects of sexual development.

Social Learning Theory

The leading proponent of social learning theory, which emphasizes the importance of role models and significant adults in young children's lives, was Albert Bandura (born in 1925). Bandura proposed that human beings are not simply passive receivers of information and experiences, but use sophisticated thinking to draw on past experiences, think about the consequences of their behavior, and anticipate future possibilities. As infants and children become *socialized* within their families and cultural groups, their own unique characteristics, behaviors, and levels of understanding affect how they respond to people and events. But the unique characteristics of an infant's social environment equally affect the infant. Unlike age/stage theories, social learning theory suggests that the course of development for any child depends on the kinds of social learning experiences encountered. The child's responses and interactions change over time as she matures and her social experiences expand.

Definition: *Socialization*—the process by which children acquire the accepted behaviors and values of their families and society.

Erikson's Theory of Emotional/Social Development

Like Freud, Erik Erikson (1902–1994) believed that development moves through a series of stages that we can recognize. He examined the emotional and social interactions between children and their caregivers, and he believed that early experiences affected later personality development. But unlike Freud, Erikson was interested in the larger cultural and societal setting in which emotional and social development takes place.

Erikson identified eight stages of emotional and social development that describe developmental changes from infancy through our adult lives.

Table 5.1: Erikson's Eight Psychosocial Stages

Birth to 1 year	Trust vs. mistrust
1 to 3 years	Autonomy vs. shame and doubt
3 to 6 years	Initiative vs. guilt
6 to 11 years	Industry vs. inferiority
Adolescent years	Identity vs. role confusion
Adult	Intimacy/solidarity vs. isolation
Adult	Generativity vs. self-absorption
Adult	Integrity (a sense of being a complete person) vs. despair

Erikson's work is important for parents and child care professionals because it shows how children develop the foundation for emotional and social development and mental health. Erikson believed that there is a task each of us must complete at each stage of development. How we complete a given stage, or fail to do so, affects the next stage. As we pass through each stage, we develop personality strengths (or weaknesses) based on what we accomplish in that stage. He also believed that we will experience conflicts, especially during our adolescent years, as we grow to become adults. (It was Erikson who invented the term *identity crisis*.) He believed that while certain tasks ideally needed to be completed at each stage for the best development, it was still possible later in life for people to work on tasks that were not successfully completed earlier in life.

According to Erikson's theory, for example, the first year of life is a very important time for infants to develop a sense of trust in themselves, in others, and in the world around them. Erikson believed that, for infants, trust has two parts: external (believing that the adults in their lives will meet their needs) and internal (believing that they have the power to bring about changes and to manage many different circumstances).

Infants learn to trust when their needs for food, comfort, and communication are met; when their lives are full of nurturing, warm, and tender interactions with parents and other caregivers; and when they have predictable routines. Infants' early experiences of being held and fed when hungry, held and stroked soothingly when sad or crying, changed when needed, protected from injury, and played with when bored all build a sense of trust. When these very basic needs are met, infants learn to trust their own ability to communicate needs and to get the attention and care they want.

On the other hand, mistrust grows when caregivers fail to respond to their hunger, discomfort, boredom, and other needs, or when they don't respond in regular and positive ways. Infants who are neglected, rejected, or often left to cry learn that other people cannot be trusted. Equally damaging, they come to believe that they have no power to affect the world around them.

When infants' basic needs are met, they learn to trust their own ability to communicate needs and to get the attention and care they want.

Erikson believed that parents and other caregivers can take two important steps to help reinforce infants' sense of trust:

1. Hold infants close and have warm physical contact with them while they are being fed.
2. Respond right away when they fuss or cry.

These warm feelings are just as important for infants' emotional health and growth as food is for their physical health and growth. Providing a positive environment for feeding time is as important in a child care setting as it is in their own home.

SPOILING BABIES

Based on Erikson's theories, babies have few coping skills, and it is the responsibility of the adults in their lives to keep them safe and comfortable. Adults in many cultures understand this. In the United States, however, many adults still believe that we spoil babies when we give them the attention they are crying for. According to Erikson's theory, babies will develop the strongest sense of security if they know that adults will come immediately when they cry. By meeting their needs quickly and consistently during this stage of their lives, parents and caregivers are doing the opposite of spoiling the child. They are actually building a strong foundation for the child to grow into a confident toddler and eventually, into a confident adult who can live an independent, happy life.

Babies who succeed in this stage enter the second year of life believing that the world is a good and safe place to be. They trust that their caregivers will take good care of them. These infants will be ready for the next stage, developing a sense of autonomy. Autonomy builds upon this basic sense of trust and emerges during the toddler stage—ages one to three.

Attachment Theory

The ideas of infant *bonding* and *attachment* have received much attention in recent years. Attachment theory was formulated by John Bowlby (1907–1990) and Mary Ainsworth (1913–1999).

Bonding refers to the strong emotional connection between the mother or father (or other caregiver) and the infant. Bonding occurs in the early days or weeks after birth. *Attachment* happens gradually during the first year, based on the quality of the interactions between the child and the parent or other primary caregiver.

Once infants begin to form attachments, they begin to recognize that not all caregivers are the same person. At this point, most, if not all, children develop *stranger anxiety* (fear of strangers) and *separation anxiety*. Signs of stranger anxiety include avoiding or hiding from strangers and/or crying when they are near.

Definition: *Separation anxiety*—the fear children have of being separated from the person they're attached to.

Separation anxiety begins to happen as the relationship between the infant and the attachment person (mother, father, or other primary caregiver) becomes more intense and exclusive. Infants will cry, sometimes quite hard, when they can't see the attachment person, and they will show intense joy when he or she returns. Although this phase can worry parents, primary caregivers, and secondary caregivers (like child care providers), it's a healthy part of the infant's growth. When adults respond to separation anxiety in supportive and kind ways, a child gains even more trust and confidence in his caregivers.

Child care professionals can be a big help to parents of infants in their care by helping them understand their infants' fears when separation anxiety occurs, and by offering suggestions on how to respond appropriately to the situation. The following list offers excellent suggestions both for parents and for other caregivers during this brief but difficult phase.

Responding Sensitively to Separation Anxiety

- Recognize that new experiences present new challenges for the infant; some of these challenges can be quite unsettling, even frightening.
- Provide predictable, easygoing schedules, particularly when introducing the infant to new experiences.
- Begin to help the infant adjust to short separations at home by maintaining visual and auditory contact by leaving the infant's door open at naptimes and bedtimes; maintaining voice contact across rooms; and, when departing the room of a protesting infant, providing softly spoken verbal assurances.
- Ritualize bedtimes and naptimes: provide a slower pace, soften the volume on the TV, give the child a bath and a change of clothing, brush her teeth, read a story, rock and sing to her, kiss her goodnight, and tuck her in bed.
- Provide a chance for the infant to become familiar with a new babysitter or child care arrangement before actually putting him in the new person's care.
- Select caregivers who will respond to the infant's unique rhythms and temperament.
- Talk with the caregiver about the infant's routines and preferences.
- Bring a special blanket, stuffed toy, or other object.
- Ritualize departure time: hug, kiss, say good-bye, wave, and so on.
- Show excitement and pleasure about the new experience.
- Be dependable. First separations should be brief, and reunions should be very predictable.

Stranger anxiety often surfaces at seven to eight months of age. When infants at this age meet or are cared for by an adult they don't know, their fear of strangers will likely be triggered. They may stare for a long time at the unknown person or burst into tears while holding tightly to the attachment person. "Responding Sensitively to Stranger Anxiety" lists a number of steps parents and other caregivers can take to lessen infants' fear of strangers. Provide this list to parents when they come to register a child in your program in order to help ease their worries *and* the child's anxiety.

The steps parents take at home can help you transition the child to your care.

Stranger anxiety, like separation anxiety, is a sign of more mature neurological, emotional, and social development. When caregivers respond to these fears with kindness and understanding, they help infants further build trust in themselves and others.

Responding Sensitively to Stranger Anxiety

Learning to understand that their parents are different from others is a big step for babies. Having to get to know another caregiver can be difficult and scary. Parents and caregivers should recognize that these fears are a natural part of new experiences.

- Don't let an unfamiliar person hold the infant without preparation.
- Provide enough time for the infant to judge the stranger and sense your reaction to her.
- When introducing the infant to a new caregiver, spend time together to give the infant a chance to accept this new person into his world.
- During this session, let yourself be a "safe base" from which the infant can begin to assess and accept the new person.
- Let the infant "control" the meeting and decide when to approach and when to move back.
- Give the infant a familiar and comforting object to hold, such as a special blanket or a stuffed animal.

Throughout our early childhood years, information coming through our senses and our interactions with others stimulate the growth of a very complex network of connections in the brain. In chapter 6, you'll learn about the connection between the child development theories you just read about and remarkable new research on brain growth. You'll also learn about two very important development factors: *windows of opportunity*, which we've already touched on in chapter 2, and *essential experiences*. You'll understand why they are so important in early brain growth and development and how you can influence them.

6 The Neurobiology of Psychosocial Development

Recent discoveries about early brain growth and neurological development now reinforce many prominent child development theories. One of the most important of these discoveries is the idea of *windows of opportunity* (discussed in chapter 2)—certain periods of growth and development during which experiences seem to have a greater effect on the changing young child. Even though people can learn new ways of thinking and behaving throughout their lives, the most significant brain development, or "neurological wiring," happens during the first three years for some developmental achievements, and continues up to seven to ten years for others. To get the most out of this special time, children must have certain experiences. For example, psychologists and other researchers have believed for many years that early bonding and attachment is very important. Today's discoveries clearly show that bonding and attachment experiences actually *change* an infant's brain in ways that do not happen with infants who do not have these experiences. And while genetics clearly affects many traits and characteristics, we humans still depend very much on our environment for the opportunity to develop as best we can. This view is also supported by research on how the human brain organizes itself.

> *Bonding and attachment experiences actually* change *an infant's brain in ways that do not happen with infants who do not have these experiences.*

Psychosocial Development: A Neurological View

Our brain controls our thinking, emotions, and behavior—including expressions of joy, love, hate, friendship, curiosity, fear, sadness, shyness, anxiety, and many other emotions—as well as the behaviors our emotions influence. Throughout our early childhood years, information coming from our senses and our interactions with others stimulates the growth of a very complex network of connections in the brain.

Much genetically controlled neurological development happens before birth. After birth, however, influences on brain development come mainly from our interactions with the world around us. Stimulation from the environment causes the brain to develop its own unique circuits, and affects which connections will last and which will go away. In some cases, connections will change because of injury or neglect. *All* the experiences a child has affect his neurological development.

During windows of opportunity, the brain is especially sensitive to environmental influences, both positive and negative, as shown in table 2.1 on page 12. During this period, certain *essential experiences* strengthen particular brain activities. Essential experiences are ones needed to stimulate and improve brain activity during early growth and development. They are the experiences and interactions that are provided by nurturing and supportive caregivers. They strengthen a child's memory and learning ability, her expression and control of emotions, and her social behaviors. In table 6.1, you'll see examples of the types of essential experiences that help healthy brain growth and neurological development.

Unfortunately, the opposite is also true. Being deprived, neglected, and/or abused during these special times can have particularly long-lasting *negative* brain effects.

Windows of opportunity open for:

- developing social attachment (birth to two years)
- learning to control or change emotions (birth to two years)
- developing the ability to cope with stress (birth to three years)

Experts in child development now believe that strong, secure attachment to a nurturing caregiver actually can provide biological "protection" for infants against the later effects of stress or trauma. In addition, neuroscientists now know that stressful or traumatic experiences in infancy and early childhood—if they continue for a long time—can actually affect neurological development and harm brain function. It's been shown that school-age children who have had secure attachment relationships during infancy and early childhood have fewer behavior problems when they experience stress or trauma.

Researchers have concluded that our ability to express and control emotions as adults is greatly affected by caring, nurturing, and supportive interactions in early childhood because their interactions stimulate and create certain connections in the brain. Early experiences actually create the biological systems that let us express or channel emotions. It follows, then, that children who have been abused, abandoned, neglected, or otherwise emotionally mistreated or neglected have less ability to control or channel their emotions appropriately than children who were raised in a supportive environment.

Strong, secure attachment to a nurturing caregiver actually can provide biological "protection" for infants against the later effects of stress or trauma.

Much of what we know about windows of opportunity was learned through animal studies. One of the first studies took place in the 1960s by a group of researchers at the University of California at Berkeley (Diamond, Krech, and Rosenzweig 1964). They examined the brain size and brain thickness of rats that had been raised in two kinds of cages: an "enriched" cage where they lived with other rats and had "toys" to play with, and a small cage without playmates or toys.

The experiments clearly showed that the rats raised in the enriched cage were much better at finding their way through mazes than the rats raised in the "boring" cage. Furthermore, the "enriched" rats actually had a thicker *cerebral cortex* than the other rats. It was thus concluded that differences in early life experiences affect the actual structure of the brain.

Definition: *Cerebral cortex*—the outer layer of the front part of the brain, which is primarily responsible for higher-level nerve functions. In humans, it is the part of the brain where self-awareness and our ability to think and reason take place.

What do these and similar studies tell us about the human brain? We now know that enriched and mentally stimulating environments increase the growth of neurons and the connections between them in humans—and they thicken the human cerebral cortex too. Scientists can trace the beginning of various types of development—vision, hearing, motor controls, language, and so on—through periods of sensitive and rapid growth when certain experiences have a greater effect—again, during windows of opportunity. While brain enrichment is possible throughout our lives, childhood and adolescence appear to be the best periods for brain development—times when neural growth and connections are most productive.

Table 6.1: **Essential Experiences in Infancy**

Developmental Domain	Essential Experiences
Social attachment and the ability to cope with stress	• Dependable care that is predictable, warm, and nurturing • Gentle, loving, and dependable relationships with primary caregivers • Immediate attention to physiological needs for food, elimination, cleanliness, warmth, exercise, and signs of illness • Satisfying and enjoyable social interactions • Playful experiences and fun infant toys
Regulation and control of emotions	• Compassionate adult responses and unconditional acceptance of the child's unique characteristics and personality traits • Adult expectations that are appropriate for the age and the individual • Leadership that helps the child learn about emotions and that suggests proper ways to express emotions and proper contexts for their expression • Relationships that are psychologically safe—free of threat, force, teasing, or physical or psychological neglect or abuse • Opportunities to take part in socially and emotionally satisfying play
Vision and auditory ability	• Regular vision and hearing examinations by health care professionals • Personal possessions, toys, and baby books that have interesting colors, shapes, textures, sizes, patterns, sounds, pitches, rhythm, and movement • Experiences with many forms of music, song, and dance
Motor development and coordination	• Opportunities and encouragement to use growing muscle coordination in safe and interesting surroundings • Play space, equipment, and toys that help both large and small muscle coordination
Vocabulary and language development	• Rich responses to the infant's efforts to communicate • Talking, chanting, singing, sharing, reading picture books, telling stories, and sharing poems and rhymes with the infant • Toys and other materials that encourage pretend play • Talking with the child about many topics using interesting vocabulary • Telling stories • Focused and responsive interactions in both native and second languages • Opportunities to converse and sing in either language

Cognitive development	• Toys and learning materials that the child can play and build with—dumping and pouring, pushing and pulling, dropping and retrieving, and hiding and finding • Toys and other materials that encourage pretend play • Social interactions that encourage exploring and play • Baby books that introduce familiar objects, labels, and simple stories • Enjoyable recorded music or pleasing instrumental music and singing

In the next chapter, we will look more closely at psychosocial growth and examine the important topics of temperament, crying as communication, and the stages in an infant's development of self-awareness.

Reference

Diamond, M. C., D. Krech, and M. R. Rosenzweig. 1964. "The effects of an enriched environment on the histology of the rat cerebral cortex." *Journal of Comparative Neurology* 123:111–119.

7 Dimensions of Psychosocial Development

Infant Temperament

From birth, infants have their own personalities, something that has sparked the curiosity of parents and researchers alike. Researchers Stella Chess and Alexander Thomas (1987, 1996) have identified three main types of temperament:

1. *The easy temperament.* These children are usually easygoing, even-tempered, accepting of change, playful, open, and adaptable. Their eating and sleeping schedules are quite regular, they are easily comforted when upset, and they often are in a good mood.
2. *The difficult temperament.* These children are slower to develop regular eating and sleeping routines, are more irritable, get less pleasure from playtime activities, have difficulty adjusting to changes in routines, and tend to cry louder and longer than children with an easy temperament.
3. *The slow-to-warm-up temperament.* These children show only mild positive or negative reactions, they don't like new situations and people, and they are moody and slow to adapt. The slow-to-warm-up child may resist close interactions such as cuddling.

The behaviors of a child with an easy temperament positively reinforce a caregiver's actions. This, of course, tends to affect the kind and amount of attention the child receives throughout early development. More often than not, these children experience what researchers call a *goodness of fit* between themselves and their caregivers. If there is goodness of fit between infants and their environment, the positive outcomes can carry over into later development and adulthood.

> Definition: *Goodness of fit*—when the child's abilities, motivations, and style of behaving fit well with the demands and expectations of his caregivers. Such a match creates a positive environment for growth and development. A poor match—*poorness of fit*—can have the opposite effect on the caregiver–child relationship and on the child's growth and development.

Temperamentally difficult infants may fail to elicit the nurturing and support they need from their caregivers. Adults who find a child's temperament hard to respond to may become punishing, overly demanding, or inconsistent in their interactions. They may be unclear with the child about expectations. The child may not feel completely loved and accepted by his caregivers. The adults may feel helpless, confused, and unable to cope with the child. They may get into power struggles for control. In such situations, a child may not develop the ability to have effective and positive relationships, and behavior problems may continue into adulthood.

Children with slow-to-warm-up temperaments generally are not too difficult to raise. Still, because they are slower to adapt to new situations and are shier about meeting new people, their caregivers may not always give the effort needed to have regular positive interactions.

Not all children fall exactly into these categories, of course. Children with easy temperaments are not always easy; children with difficult temperaments are not always difficult; and children with slow-to-warm-up temperaments are not always hesitant. Recognizing and appreciating individual differences, however, helps parents and other caregivers respond appropriately to these children.

Adults must be cautious in using labels for children. Self-fulfilling prophecies ("getting what you expect") can happen—the child behaves according to the adult's limited expectations. If adults accept the labels and misunderstand the infant's cues, they may fail to meet the infant's needs for positive and nurturing interactions, regardless of the child's temperament or personality.

If adults who care for infants can respond appropriately to the different temperaments of infants more often, the better the goodness of fit will be between infants and caregivers. Since temperament is partly genetically determined, it's the adult caregivers' responsibility to adjust to the infant's expressions of need and to provide total acceptance of the child.

Jeremy, at four months old, is usually quite content at bedtime. His mother usually holds him in her lap for a while after his evening feeding. He drifts into drowsiness and then into irregular sleep. Her soft voice hums to him while he drowses in her arms. Sensing his readiness for the crib, she carries him to his room. Placing him quietly in his crib, she continues to hum. She rubs his tummy softly and then leaves the room after seeing that he will soon fall soundly to sleep.

However, on this particular evening, Jeremy doesn't want to sleep. His eyes are open and he's looking around the room, though he seems tired and cries a little. Tonight, he's a bit fussy. His mother, also tired, wishes that some magic formula would soothe him and help him to rest. Nevertheless, after deciding that Jeremy is not hungry, his diaper does not need changing, and his clothing is comfortable, she follows her usual routine. After being placed in his crib, he looks around and cries a little while Ann rubs his tummy gently. Though he has not fallen into sound sleep, she leaves the room.

Angela is less easily calmed than Jeremy. At bedtime, she's fretful and restless. Noticing from the usual afternoon and evening family routines that bedtime is near, she begins to whimper and cry. She doesn't want to be held or comforted.

Angela's grandmother, sensing a difficult bedtime, goes to her. She carries Angela on her shoulder as she walks around the house giving cleanup and bedtime instructions to the other children. Patting a fussy Angela, she continues to walk, talk, and hush the baby. When this doesn't work, she goes to a back bedroom. Away from the rest of the family, she places Angela across her lap and begins to sing and talk softly to her. For a time, Angela still wiggles, lifts her head, and frets. She is easily distracted by the sound of children playing inside the house. Her grandmother continues to sing and talk or hum until at last Angela begins to rest and finally falls asleep.

Crying: An Important Way Infants Communicate

Infants first communicate their needs through crying. It's important to understand that infants have no real control over their crying and will not be able to stop until a need has been met or they become too tired to cry. As infants get older, the reasons they cry—such as loud noises, physical restraint, uncomfortable clothing, frustration with toys, or fear of strangers or separation—begin to change.

WHY SOME CHILDREN CRY MORE THAN OTHERS

As any parent or caregiver knows, crying can be very bothersome, particularly when you can't figure out what the infant needs. One key to caregiving is learning to tell what an infant's different cries mean and to respond quickly. Much research shows that infants whose parents responded quickly to their cries and other signals cried less often and for a shorter time. The opposite is also true; infants who cried and fussed the most after three months of age had parents who didn't respond quickly to their cries. Other research shows that infants who were held and carried during the day cried less during the night.

As with older children and adults, infants can feel bored or lonely, and need personal contact. Sometimes crying simply means they need company, the sound of a familiar voice, or the feel of a familiar touch. When bored, infants may cry just for a change of position or place, or just to be closer to others.

It is important to understand that infants have no real control over their crying, and they won't be able to stop until a need has been met or they become too tired to cry.

SOCIAL SMILING AND FACIAL EXPRESSIONS

At first, infants smile at faces regardless of facial expression. Then, from three to seven months, they begin to notice and respond to differences in facial expressions. In the latter part of the first year, infants not only can see differences in facial expressions, they can respond to individual expressions in different emotional ways. Infants can respond to positive and negative tones in the human voice (e.g., smiling more when they hear sounds of approval than when they hear sounds of disapproval), as well as to facial and bodily expressions of their caregivers. As infants get older, they become more skilled at reading expression and body language (especially in their caregivers). They begin to use these cues to guide their own behavior. For example, they become more picky about smiling, choosing to smile more at familiar faces, voices, and interactions.

Self-Awareness

As we noted in our discussion on attachment, infants find it frightening when they first begin to realize that they are separate from other humans.

But to truly participate in the give-and-take of a relationship, an infant must first develop a sense of being separate and apart from others. Emotions such as love, hate, jealousy, and guilt—the types of complex emotions that appear in relationships with others—are related to our sense of self.

Most child development researchers believe that there are five stages in infants' growing awareness that they are separate from others:

1. Birth to three months: Interactions between infants and their caregivers and objects are instinctive rather than thoughtful.
2. Three to eight months: Thanks to more and more interactions with others, infants begin to sense a growing difference between themselves and others, though they may not make a distinction in all situations.
3. Eight to twelve months: The distinction between themselves and others is quite clear. Infants see themselves as different and permanent in time and space.
4. Twelve to eighteen months: Feelings and emotions such as self-consciousness, embarrassment, and separation anxiety begin to emerge, along with an ability to recognize themselves in a mirror or photo.
5. Eighteen to thirty months: Self-definition begins to emerge; toddlers are now aware enough of themselves to begin to talk about their age, gender, and other characteristics.

This growing self-awareness depends on sufficient cognitive development to allow the child to make certain mental distinctions, such as being able to tell the difference between "like me" and "not like me."

Children's self-awareness also depends on their social experiences. Infants are able to begin to develop their sense of self by being with others and seeing how others respond to them. These self-concepts change continually as new abilities emerge and their social world grows to include more and more people than just their primary caregivers.

In chapter 8, we'll focus on the factors that affect a child's development, including the role of early childhood professionals in promoting psychosocial development in infants.

References

Chess, S., and A. Thomas. 1987. *Origins and evolution of behavior disorders: from infancy to early adult life*. Cambridge, Mass.: Harvard University Press.

———. 1996. *Temperament: Theory and practice*. New York: Brunner/Mazel.

8 Factors Influencing Psychosocial Development

Quality and Consistency of Care

Three of the most important qualities of infant care for healthy psychological, emotional, and social development are *consistency*, *predictability*, and *continuity* of care. Though caregivers' personalities and responses may differ somewhat, infants need caregivers such as their mother, father, siblings, and child care providers to respond to their needs in relatively similar and nurturing ways. Early experiences that provide predictable routines, feeding, and tender closeness, along with dependable and timely responses to needs, build a sense of trust that is important to healthy psychological, emotional, and social development.

Success and Quality of Bonding and Attachment

Bonding and attachment experiences significantly affect the way infants' brains process social and emotional information and how they become "wired" for a positive (or negative) outlook on life. These experiences have effects on social and emotional development, and even on the development of moral values during later childhood, the teen years, and adulthood.

Essential Experiences

Essential experiences (see table 6.1), which take place during special periods of brain growth and development, are simple and usually come naturally, but they also can be strengthened intentionally by infants' care-givers. Early experiences that promote the best early brain growth and neurological development also help protect against later stress and increase a child's learning abilities.

Social and Cultural Experiences and Relationships

Because the first influences on child growth and development happen within a small group of people (primary caregivers such as parents, older siblings, grandparents, or guardians; and secondary caregivers such as child care professionals, friends, or neighbors), a child's cultural heritage and environment have a dramatic effect on his development. Social contacts that let infants watch and imitate positive and supportive behaviors of others in their family and in their cultural groups help them learn useful social skills. Learning to read facial expressions, body language, and other cues helps infants notice and manage their own feelings and behaviors.

As noted in our discussion of cultural influences in chapter 1, culture affects psychological, emotional, and social development through learned perceptions, values, goals, and expectations about child rearing. Expression of emotions, expectations, encouragement of infant responses, acceptance of infant behaviors, and the role of parents vary both among cultures and within them. Attitudes toward feeding, crying, holding, clothing, language, sickness and health, medicine, and social services, as well as religious belief systems and many other issues, greatly affect infants' psychological, emotional, and social development.

Social and economic levels also play a role in development, especially in families who are poor. For some (though certainly not all) families living in extreme poverty, survival needs often come before the social and emotional needs of children and before the physiological needs for adequate nutrition, health care, and medication. The challenge just to survive, and the stress of poverty in general, can be so overwhelming that they interfere with healthy parent-parent and parent-child interactions. Parents may not be able to provide food, clothing, shelter, and transportation for the family. Children in such families may be hungry and/or cold, suffer more frequent illnesses, and even be neglected or abused. Tiredness, frustration, worry, and anger or loss of hope can prevent parents from being able to meet the psychological, emotional, and social needs of their children.

For such families, high-quality child care can provide much-needed support. Child care professionals also may be able to provide access to social and health care services, job counseling, and parenting education. By having access to full days of nurturing and supportive interactions, infants have a better chance for healthy development. Relief from the stress of parenting and knowing that their child is well cared for during the day (or night) can be a great relief for parents in these difficult situations.

While there are excellent resources for disadvantaged families—such as Head Start for preschoolers and public child care assistance programs for parents receiving public assistance or for low-income working parents—a number of these families don't know how to get access to these programs, many of which are underfunded and have long waiting lists. For some cultural groups, there's also a resistance to seeking help outside the family or ethnic circle. Many children end up being cared for by relatives or neighbors who do unlicensed home care with mixed results. The much-needed quality support during the crucial first months of a child's development may or may not be provided.

Psychological Factors: Infant Mental Health

The environment in which an infant grows and is nurtured, along with her inherited physical and psychological characteristics, affect her mental health. As she grows, a number of social and psychological skills also contribute to her mental health, including whether she:

- develops a sense of trust in herself and others
- forms secure attachments
- learns to control her emotions
- gets attention and interacts with others
- communicates emotions, such as discomfort, pain, contentment, and joy
- lets caregivers help and comfort her
- learns to talk, and then to communicate her needs and feelings

This developmental process is very much affected by the quality of the relationships infants form in their family and home environments, child care settings, and community. Infants' relationships with key people in these arenas can help or harm their mental, emotional, and social development. This growth depends on caregivers who are quick to respond and nurturing, who understand infants' needs and behavior, and recognize when behaviors may be the sign of a mental health problem. When such problems arise, they know to get professional help.

Psychological and emotional problems in infants and young children are difficult to identify because many behaviors (temper tantrums, nervousness, and disobeying caregivers, for example) are, to some degree, normal. And they are usually temporary, changing as the child matures or as her needs are met. (See table 4.1, "When to Worry about At-Risk Infants and Toddlers.")

While few events can actually cause mental problems or disorders, certain risk factors can make these problems more likely. These include:

- prenatal damage from exposure to alcohol, illegal drugs, and tobacco
- low birth weight
- a difficult temperament
- inherited predisposition to a mental disorder
- poverty
- deprivation
- abuse
- neglect
- a parent with a mental health disorder
- substance dependence in one or more caregivers
- exposure to traumatic events
- exposure to toxic chemicals in the house or yard

Growing up in a problem-filled family environment also puts children at risk. These problems include:

- parents who don't get along and who fight often
- parents who have problems with mental illness, substance abuse, or criminal behavior
- overcrowded living conditions or large family size
- problems with siblings
- exposure to violence or criminal activity
- poverty (which increases the risk of child abuse)

Whether a risk factor will have a negative effect on one child but not on another depends on:

- individual differences in children
- the age when the child experiences the problem or trauma
- how strong the trauma is and how long it lasts
- the type and timeliness of help

Infants who experience chronic illnesses, birth defects, injury, violence, emotionally unstable caregivers, or inconsistent child-rearing practices are most likely to have emotional, social, and psychological problems at some point in their lives. Of course, the sooner children receive help for a mental problem, the more likely the treatment will succeed. Treatment options can include family counseling and support programs, psychotherapy, medications, and special residential treatment programs.

Watch for Signs of Stress

When infants are having problems, they tend to show signs of stress physically. Caregivers may see:

- changes in sleeping and waking patterns
- problems with feeding and eating
- more intense emotions
- frantic or nonstop crying
- depression-like behavior
- loss of interest in interacting or playing with caregivers or other children

When caregivers notice these kinds of behaviors, they should take a close look at the family or child care situation. Again, professional counseling may be needed to help the family cope with their difficulties and to respond appropriately to the infant.

Interactions That Build Social Awareness and Skills

Social contacts that let infants watch and imitate positive and supportive behaviors of others in their family, child care settings, and cultural groups foster positive mental health and help infants learn useful social skills. Learning to read facial expressions, body language, and other cues also helps infants notice and manage their own feelings and behaviors.

A child's personality certainly affects the number and types of interactions he has with others. Still, the more often adults who care for infants can respond appropriately to the different temperaments of infants, the better the goodness of fit will be between infants and caregivers. Since temperament is partly genetically determined, it's the adult caregivers' responsibility to adjust to the infant's expressions of need and to provide total acceptance of the child.

Cheryl's mother finds it difficult to work a full-time job and help Cheryl care for Angela. The older kids in Cheryl's family also help with babysitting, but they are still children themselves, with schoolwork to do and the desire and need to play and interact with peers.

Cheryl, who is still attending school, feels pressured to find new child care arrangements. A family friend informs Cheryl that some high schools in the area have on-site child care for teenage mothers. Cheryl's mother locates one of these schools, but in order for Cheryl to attend, the family will have to move. Cheryl doesn't want to move, but feels she has no choice.

During this time, Angela, at eight months old, is experiencing irregular sleeping patterns and other issues, due in part to the constant change of caregivers. She is hungry at odd hours and is a picky eater. She cries easily and often, always wants someone with her, and strongly fights going to bed. She responds easily to Cheryl and to Cheryl's mother, but frets or cries when left in her playpen as others leave the room. Both Cheryl and her mother care deeply for Angela and want her to be a happy, cheerful baby. They decide to move so that Cheryl can attend the high school with on-site child care, which they hope will provide a stable, predictable, and caring environment for Angela.

Jeremy's experiences have been quite different from Angela's. His world has included his mother, his father, Phyllis (his babysitter), an occasional visit from grandparents, and trips to the church nursery. Except for some problems with stomach pain, Jeremy's sleeping and eating routines are generally problem free. Bathing, dressing, and playing with Phyllis and his parents are most often relaxed, predictable, and enjoyable events.

Ann, now back at work outside the home, is doing everything she can to keep a sense of order at home, though meeting Jeremy's needs at times overwhelms her. Ann and Bill talk often about the huge change Jeremy has made in their lifestyle, daily schedules, social life, and physical stamina.

Since birth, Jeremy's routines have mostly been regular and happy. The adults in his world respond to his needs, his sense of trust is emerging, and he has learned which cries and motions will get him what he needs. At eight months old, he's beginning to be upset when he's separated from his parents or from Phyllis. He's especially suspicious of strangers and seems to need more close physical contact than usual. He cries more frequently than he used to, and is especially difficult in the morning, when Ann and Bill are rushing to dress and leave for work.

Continuity of Care

Studies have shown that the fewer caregivers infants have, the more secure they feel in the early stages of their emotional and social development. For this reason, many child care centers today provide a dedicated caregiver for infants as a way to reduce the number of adults an infant must adapt to. This helps the infant's sense of order and makes it easier to form positive relationships and healthy attachments with nonparental caregivers.

In the stories about Angela and Jeremy, both infants receive nonparental care while their parents are away from home. Angela's routines are less predictable than Jeremy's, because her caregivers change so often. The inconsistency of care she is receiving has given her less of a chance than Jeremy has to develop stable, trusting relationships.

Nonparental Child Care

It has become commonplace today for parents to use nonparental child care for their infants, many beginning as early as six weeks of age. These arrangements can include care by a member of the child's family (grandparent, aunt, uncle, cousin, older sibling), a neighbor, an in-home babysitter, a professional family child care provider, or a child care center with an infant/toddler program. Probably the biggest question parents with young children in child care have is, "Will my child develop normally being away from her parents at such an early age?" Much research has been done to address this question. Some studies showed that, at first, infants in child care programs were less outgoing, but this effect seemed to go away after six months or so. The children then behaved similarly to children who were cared for in a home setting. These studies also showed that when caregivers were very responsive and comforting to infants when they first came to the care setting, over the next six months, the infants' upset behaviors gradually went away. This study also suggested that it takes three to six months for infants to feel comfortable in child care settings. With poor-quality care, however, the adjustment period can be longer. While some studies suggest that long hours (twenty or more per week) in nonparental child care can slow the development of secure attachments between infants and their mothers, others do not agree.

THE KEY FACTOR: THE QUALITY OF THE CHILD CARE

Nearly all research shows that the most important factor is the quality of the child care setting and staff. Quality infant care programs have staff who are very involved with the children and who provide developmentally proper care. They have low infant-to-caregiver/teacher ratios and small groups (the younger the child, the smaller the group should be). The same holds true for home care settings. The fewer the children and the more attention the provider can give to each infant, the better the prospects for each child.

Earlier, we talked about the importance of a parent's or other primary caregiver's sensitivity and responsiveness to an infant's cues and needs. Clearly, the same holds true for professional providers. Stressing the importance of high-quality child care programs, an important study by Helen Raikes focused on how the amount of time an infant spends in the care of a "high-ability" teacher affects infant-teacher attachment.

Because a secure attachment with a caring and nurturing caregiver can ease the stress of parental separation, such an attachment is very important. These child-caregiver attachments can even compensate for insecure parental attachments.

Raikes' study (1993) showed the following:

- High-ability caregivers/teachers do help infants' developing sense of trust, predictability, and control.
- With time, child care staff can get to know the infants' personalities and what upsets, excites, amuses, and bores them.
- It takes time for secure attachments to develop.
- Quality relationships foster successful cognitive, social, emotional, and language development in infants.
- Being able to spend at least nine months with the same provider provides the best chance for an infant to form a secure attachment.

Raikes also suggested that rather than "promoting" infants at age six or seven months, which is quite common in child care programs, a new standard for excellence in the field would keep infants and high-ability teachers together beyond one year of age.

Communication between parents and caregivers is also important in nonparental child care. Studies show that the more communication parents had with child care staff, the better the care their child received.

Characteristics of high-quality child care are:

- trained, knowledgeable, nurturing, and dedicated caregivers
- a safe, sanitary, healthy environment for infants and children
- low adult-child ratios, with an emphasis on providing dedicated caregivers to individual infants over extended periods of time
- environments and caregivers that are cognitively and linguistically enriching, socially stimulating, and emotionally supportive

- sensitive and appropriate interactions and activities for all children
- sensitivity to parents' needs, goals, and concerns
- exceeding of local and/or state licensing standards
- accreditation through the National Association for the Education of Young Children or other nationally recognized accrediting agency

Reference

Raikes, H. 1993. "Relationship duration in infant care: Time with a high-ability teacher and infant-teacher attachment." *Early Childhood Research Quarterly* 8, no. 3:309–25.

The Role of the Early Childhood Professional

1. Provide warm, loving, supportive, predictable, consistent, and continuous care
2. Respond readily to the infant's cues for food, comfort, rest, play, and social interaction
3. Recognize that crying is the infant's way of communicating needs
4. Be aware of sensitive periods relating to attachment behaviors, separation, and stranger anxiety, and respond in supportive and empathic ways
5. Be aware of windows of opportunity and the need for certain essential experiences to promote optimal brain growth and neurological development
6. Provide stimulating and satisfying social and emotional interactions
7. Respond readily to the infant's playful overtures
8. Recognize and accept the infant's unique temperament and ways of interacting with others
9. Recognize and respond in accepting and supportive ways to the infant's various emotional displays

Discussion Questions

1. How do you respond when a child in your care shows signs of separation anxiety? Do you offer response strategies to parents of children in your care? How do your strategies compare with those suggested in chapter 5?
2. Chapter 6 discusses the role a stimulating and nurturing environment plays in the brain growth of infants and young children. What modifications can you or have you made to your physical setting to provide such an environment for the infants in your care? What types of infant activities and interactions do you offer?
3. Make a list of individual personality traits of the infants in your care. Which traits do you find yourself responding negatively to most often? Do you unconsciously label particular infants as "difficult" or "easy"? Talk with parents and other caregivers and share ideas about ways to positively interact with infants with challenging temperaments.
4. How many different caregivers are there for the infants in your child care setting? If there are many, what strategies does your program use to prevent frequent turnover of caregivers and/or to provide stability of care for the infants? If you are a lone caregiver in an in-home setting, what methods do you use to help infants bond with you and feel secure? How do you know if an infant has bonded with you?

Further Reading

Brazelton, T. B., and Joshua Sparrow. 2003. *Calming your fussy baby: The Brazelton way*. Reading, Mass.: Perseus.

Brazelton, T. B., and S. I. Greenspan. 2000. *The irreducible needs of children: What every child must have to grow, learn, and flourish*. Cambridge, Mass.: Perseus.

Gandini, L., and C. P. Edwards. 2000. *Bambini: The Italian approach to infant/toddler care*. New York: Teachers College Press.

Greenspan, S. I., and Serena Wieder, with Robin Simons. 1998. *The child with special needs: Encouraging intellectual and emotional growth*. New York: Perseus.

Herschkowitz, N., and E. C. Herschkowitz. 2004. *A good start in life: Understanding your child's brain and behavior*. Washington, D.C.: Dana Press.

Honig, A. S. 2002. *Secure relationships: Nurturing infant/toddler attachment in early care settings*. Washington, D.C.: National Association for the Education of Young Children.

Shore, R. 2002. *What kids need: Today's best ideas for nurturing, teaching, and protecting young children*. Boston: Beacon Press.

Part Three

Cognitive, Language, and Literacy Development

Nature has plainly not entrusted the determination of our intellectual capacities to the blind fate of a gene or genes; she gave us parents, learning, language, culture and education to program ourselves with.

—MATT RIDLEY

Infants come into the world with an amazing ability to take in all kinds of information, from the look and smell of their birth mother and the sound of her voice, to feelings of warmth and security or pain and stress. Over the first few months, parents and other caregivers see infants' skills grow. Infants quickly become curious and occupied with the world around them; they begin to communicate with and relate to others; and they become active explorers. In parts 1 and 2 of this book, we focused on infants' physical and motor development, and then on their psychological, emotional, and social development. In part 3, we will explore infants' cognitive development and their emerging language skills as they build a foundation for literacy in the months and years ahead.

9 Theories of Cognitive Development

Over the years, child development researchers cultivated four main theories about infant cognitive development. They are:

- cognitive/developmental
- information processing
- social/interactionist
- contextualist

Many parts of these theories are supported by new and exciting discoveries about the biology of the brain (called *neurobiology*). Neurobiologists are helping us understand how the structure of the brain and the ways it takes in information affect learning and memory. They also help us understand how infants can take in, organize, and understand new experiences as they develop language skills and truly begin to learn how to think.

Piaget's Theory of Cognitive Development

The most famous theory of cognitive development is that of Swiss-born psychologist Jean Piaget (1896–1980). His research had one primary goal: to understand how children learn. Piaget's studies of cognitive development have dominated the fields of child study, psychology, and education since the 1920s. As you will see, other theorists have questioned or changed Piaget's theory, but his ideas still have great influence on early childhood education.

One of Piaget's most important ideas was that young children think and solve problems quite differently than older children and adults. As caregivers, it is important to understand these differences so that you can respond to and interact with infants and young children in ways that will best support their cognitive development.

One of Piaget's most important ideas was that young children think and solve problems quite differently than older children and adults.

FOUR STAGES OF COGNITIVE DEVELOPMENT

According to Piaget's theory, there are four major stages of cognitive development: the *sensorimotor stage* (birth to age two), the *preoperational thought* (ages two to seven), *concrete operational thought* (ages seven to eleven), and the *formal operational thought* (age eleven and beyond). In the table below, you can see a summary of these stages and how they can affect what happens in child care and early education. In this section, we will look only at the sensorimotor period of infancy. Remembering the names of these stages is not as important as understanding the process of infants' cognitive development and how you as a caregiver can help and support that development.

Table 9.1: Piaget's Stages of Cognitive Development

Stages/Ages	Characteristics	Implications for Interactions and Education
I. 0 to 2 years *Sensorimotor stage*		
1. Reflexive (0 to 1 month)	Uses instinctive reflex responses	Interact in ways that stimulate the infant's sense of touch, taste, sight, sound, and smell
2. Primary circular reactions (1 to 4 months)	Repeats actions that previously happened by chance; reflexes become more coordinated	Provide sensory-stimulating toys and objects such as rattles, mobiles, baby books, recorded familiar voices, or pleasing music

3. Secondary circular reactions (4 to 10 months)	Intentionally repeats behaviors or enjoyable actions; the idea of object permanence (an object exists even when the infant can't see it) emerges	Provide clean, safe objects and toys; play hide and seek; continue to talk or sing when moving out of the child's auditory or visual field; play repetitive games
4. Coordination of secondary schemes (10 to 12 months)	Applies previously learned behaviors and activities to new situations; copying behaviors begin	Provide familiar toys, dolls, stuffed animals, blankets, and clothing; encourage imitation; provide encouraging comments
5. Tertiary circular reactions (12 to 18 months)	Cause-and-effect discoveries; seeks proximity and playful interactions with persons to whom attachments have been formed; repeats novel experiences	Respond positively to attempts to interact; provide toys that stack, nest, roll, open, close, are easily manipulated, and can be pushed or pulled; talk, label, and pretend with child
6. Symbolic representation (18 months to 2 years)	Applies learned skills to new situations; begins to think before acting; experiments with new uses for familiar objects; represents objects or events through imagery	Provide verbal labels for objects and events; encourage (and provide props [blocks, Legos, etc.] for) pretend play; provide social interaction with other children; encourage (and provide props and safe equipment for) large motor activity
II. 2 to 7 years *Preoperational thought*	Sees the world only from their point of view, ideas based on their perceptions; can focus only on one variable at a time; overgeneralizes based on limited experience	Provide a) props and toys for imaginative play and exploration; b) materials for construction (such as crayons, clay, blocks); and c) a variety of opportunities for talk, story, music, and pretend. Encourage choices and decision making; engage in extended, meaningful dialogue; encourage new experiences

III. 7 to 11 years *Concrete operational thought*	Solves basic problems with physical objects; changes their ideas; thinking is based on prior experience; the ability to remember emerges, as does simple logic	Provide opportunity to pursue areas of interest; help to obtain materials and resources for exploring and learning; encourage and show interest in school and other activities and accomplishments; engage in meaningful dialogue; use questions to extend understanding
IV. 11 years to adulthood *Formal operational thought*	Develops and tests hypotheses; uses abstract thinking; uses deductive reasoning; thinking is no longer perception bound; uses logic	Challenge with hypothetical problems to solve; discuss ethical issues; encourage and support educational interests, hobbies, and other abilities; encourage appropriate and enjoyable social interactions

According to Piaget, children's cognitive development happens one stage at a time. Piaget believed that one stage always follows another in the same way, and that each stage builds on the accomplishments of the one before it. Every child goes through these stages, but at their own speed. Differences in the timing of entering and leaving each stage are affected by individual genetic differences and cultural and environmental factors. A child who has books and whose caregivers often read to her, for example, will likely begin to read much sooner than a child who has no books and is never read to.

Piaget believed that children build their knowledge first by experiencing the world, and then by giving meaning (to the degree they can) to the people, things, and places they experience. He also believed that children need many chances to discover things for themselves. A teacher might, for example, talk about drawing and show students beautiful pictures by excellent artists. But by giving children paints, brushes, and paper so they can create their own art, they will learn much more about how to draw than any instructor could give them in words. Piaget's ideas challenged how we teach. He believed that children are by nature very curious, and that the best step preschools can take to help them learn is to support that curiosity and give them real problems to solve. For Piaget, a teacher's job is not just to give out information, but to create a learning environment that supports stu-

For Piaget, a teacher's job is not just to give out information, but to create a learning environment that supports students' curiosity and their search for answers to their questions.

dents' curiosity and their search for answers to their questions. By imitating what adults do, they begin to make sense of the world.

SENSORIMOTOR LEARNING

The sensorimotor stage continues from birth to the time when infants begin to speak and move parts of their bodies to communicate with their caregivers. During this time, infants' cognitive development depends on exploring the world with all their senses through *sensorimotor learning*: tasting, touching, feeling, hearing, and seeing. Piaget believed that a child's development of thinking abilities begins with the very early reflex and motor activities. As infants are able to better control their bodies and reflexes, movements start to have a purpose. (See the crayon, pick up the crayon, taste the crayon, draw on the freshly painted wall!) One of the best things parents and other caregivers can do for children at this age is create an interesting and safe environment that they can explore.

> Definition: *Sensorimotor learning*—learning that happens through the five senses and through physical activities.

Starting at birth, infants begin to form mental structures, which Piaget named *schemata*, by exploring the environment. These schemata help the infant mentally organize and understand their experiences. Each new experience forms new schemata or builds on existing ones. Infants' knowledge of the world grows through experiences with other people too. Piaget described infants at this stage as *egocentric*, meaning that they can only see the world and others from the perspective of their own needs and experiences.

According to Piaget, as we grow, we must learn to change and *adapt* to the world around us. When infants try to fit new ideas and concepts into existing ones, they must take in and learn new schemata. For example, at first, infants simply watch the things and people around them, and their hands and arms have only reflex activity. Later, they learn to coordinate their eyes and hands. These more coordinated responses and movements help infants interact with the objects and people around them. Each new experience changes the infant's schemata and leads to new learning. New learning builds on previous actions, events, or experiences.

Definition: *Adaptation*—developing new behaviors and skills to help in adjusting to new conditions or changes in the world.

Accommodation happens when infants change a schemata (an experience or concept) to include or adapt to a new experience. For example, the breast-fed infant who is changed from breast-feeding (existing schema) to bottle-feeding (new experience) must change his sucking behavior to succeed with the new experience, the bottle. This changed sucking behavior is an example of accommodation.

The Six Substages of the Sensorimotor Stage

The sensorimotor stage is divided into six substages. During their first year, infants move through the first four substages:

1. *Reflexive period* (birth to one month). During this period, reflexes in place since birth begin to change as the infant has new experiences.
2. *Primary circular reactions* (one to four months). At this time, infants' reactions focus on bodily responses, and they begin to have a reason for their actions. For example, an infant can now bring her thumb to her mouth to suck. Until this time, thumb sucking happened only by accident. This period is called "primary" because of its focus on bodily responses; it is called "circular" because infants repeat activities over and over again.
3. *Secondary circular reactions* (four to ten months). During this period, infants begin to focus even more on objects and events in the environment. This period is called "secondary circular" because it involves infants' growing awareness of things and events outside their bodies. At this time, infants begin to learn by chance that they can make things happen to objects. For example, when an infant hits the bath water, a big splash happens. This new experience is exciting and he wants to do it again and again and again! Also during this stage, infants will look for a hidden object. Before this time, Piaget believed, objects an infant couldn't see did not exist in the infant's mind. (This is why infants have separation anxiety—when the caregiver leaves the room, the infant believes he or she no longer exists.)
4. *Coordination of secondary schemes* (ten to twelve months).

During this time, it is obvious that infants are doing things with a purpose. Imitating other people's actions shows that the infant can now learn by watching others. He also finally realizes that objects exist even though they can't be touched or seen (object permanence).

Piaget's theory is sometimes criticized because his writing and ideas are often hard to translate and to test with research. Nevertheless, his theories are still very important for caregivers and teachers for several reasons:

- He talks about how cognitive growth and development take place in particular stages.
- He emphasizes that the way young children think is quite different from how older children and adults think.
- He emphasizes how important it is for young children to have many direct experiences with objects and people (as opposed to being placed in front of a TV for many hours each day, for example).
- He helped us better understand many parts of cognitive development, including the development of cause-and-effect relationships; time, space, and number concepts; logic; morality; and language.

Other Important Theories

While Piaget's theory of child development is the most well known, three other theories can also help parents and other caregivers better understand infants' cognitive development.

INFORMATION PROCESSING THEORY

This theory says that:

- Humans are biologically ready to recognize the world in certain ways.
- These abilities are present at birth.
- Other abilities appear in the first few months of infancy in all but the most abnormal situations.

This theory also says that while we all perceive the world through our senses, infant learning depends on three functions:

- attending: deciding what object, event, or action the infant will focus on
- identifying: deciding what an object or perception is by relating or comparing it to something already in the infant's memory
- locating: deciding where the object is

SOCIAL INTERACTIONIST THEORY

Social interactionist theories put less emphasis for learning on developmental stages and more emphasis on the importance of social situations, role models, and other environmental influences. Social interactionists believe, for example, that outside influences, such as rewards and punishments, have a greater effect on learning than the abilities infants are born with or their biological processes. They also believe that imitation plays a very large role in cognitive development. Many infant behaviors, they say, are learned simply by watching others, and much learning occurs in social situations.

CONTEXTUALIST THEORY

Contextualist theory says that development and social interaction affect one another. In other words, growing and developing children affect and are affected by the world around them. Thinking, language, and reading development are influenced by the social and cultural environment in which children grow and develop. Development in all areas depends on interactions between the individual and a variety of social and cultural influences. Contextualist theory also says that development advances to some degree in all areas at that same time. The amount of influence and the rate of development in various development areas depend on how the infant's environment affects her, as well as the temperament and responses of the infant at the time.

Jeremy, lying in his crib, is closely watching a yellow soft-sculpture airplane hanging above him. He kicks and screams with excitement, then stops and stares at the object bouncing above his crib. Lying still, he seems to notice that the object stopped swinging; when he kicks some more, the object begins to swing again. He loves this little game and repeats it several times.

Phyllis, Jeremy's babysitter, notices his interest in the plane and understands that Jeremy has discovered the link between his own body movements and the jiggling of the airplane. She comes over to his crib, unhooks the airplane, and holds it close to him, saying, "Do you want to hold the airplane? I think you like this bright toy, Jeremy."

70

Distracted from what he was just doing, Jeremy stops kicking. He stares at the soft toy, looks at Phyllis in a puzzled manner, then looks back at the toy. His eyes then travel to the hook above where the airplane had been, then back to Phyllis and the toy in her hand. He reaches for the airplane, grabs it, brings it to his mouth for a second, then drops it. Then he starts kicking the bed again and watching the space where the mobile had been hanging. Somehow things aren't the same, and he begins to cry.

In this vignette, Jeremy, six months old, is exhibiting secondary circular reactions (substage 3). The kicking that caused the airplane to bounce and swing was entertaining for him, and he was discovering that his actions could make the airplane wiggle. It's easy to want to play with playful infants, and Phyllis could not resist getting involved, but when she did, Jeremy had to make a somewhat difficult choice. He could reach for and hold the toy airplane, interact with Phyllis, or continue kicking and watching the plane move.

Though her idea about what would please Jeremy at that moment wasn't correct, Phyllis did help Jeremy's cognitive development by noticing what held his attention, naming the object, and bringing it within his reach.

Angela, at eight months old, is in her high chair. She has some difficulty sitting alone and slides under the tray, only to be caught by the high-chair safety strap between her legs. Cracker crumbs are everywhere—in her hair, in her eyebrows, between her fingers, on her clothes, and sprinkled on the floor on both sides of her chair. James and Cheryl, sitting at the table nearby, have just finished dinner and are arguing.

Angela, still stuck under the high-chair tray, starts crying. James roughly pulls her back into a seated position and continues his emotional talk with Cheryl. Angela continues to cry. Cheryl tosses another cracker on the tray while talking with James. Quiet for a moment, Angela bangs the cracker on the tray, holds what is left of it over the floor, and watches the cracker fall to the floor. Sliding under her tray again, she starts to cry, more loudly this time. Cheryl pulls her back to a seated position, but this does not comfort or quiet her. James, tired of arguing and quite distracted by the baby's crying, decides to leave.

Frustrated and angry, Cheryl picks up Angela, scolds her about the mess, takes her to the sink to wash her face and hands, then puts her in her playpen, even though Angela is still fussing. Unable to

71

respond to Angela's needs because her own needs are overwhelming, Cheryl turns on the TV, puts her feet up on the coffee table, and sinks into her sad feelings.

Unable to get her mother's attention, Angela cries awhile longer. Defeated and tired, she picks up her blanket, puts her thumb in her mouth, watches her mother, and listens to the sounds of the television set until she finally falls asleep.

Angela's reactions of frustration are natural, as she is deprived of attention and recognition of her developmental needs. For Cheryl, Angela's uncooperativeness and fussiness are more than she can deal with as she tries to cope with her own unmet needs. Cheryl's response only further deprives Angela of the essential support required for her ongoing optimal, cognitive, and emotional development.

In chapter 10, you'll learn more about the "language" of infancy and see how the ability to read and write has its roots in a number of infant experiences. You'll also learn more about the key role early childhood professionals can play in promoting cognitive, language, and literacy development in infants.

10

Factors Influencing Cognitive, Language, and Literacy Development

Earlier, we described the rapid brain growth and development that takes place in very young children. In fact, during the first ten years, a child's brain will form literally *trillions* of connections (called synapses). Rapid growth in the brain happens together with the development of hearing, language, and a better understanding of space and time information. At the same time, all the new connections in infants' brains help them better sort and understand all types of information. Growth in the brain's speech center speeds the development of speech and language.

As we've learned, the structure and functions of the neurological system are greatly affected by the interaction of infants' experiences and their genetically programmed growth and development. The quality of infants' first relationships with others is very important in early brain growth, which includes thinking, language, and literacy development. Human connections truly shape the neural connections from which infants' minds emerge (Siegel 1999).

These relationships (especially the early attachment relationships) and emotional communication affect the brain's biochemistry and wiring—they inform the neurological patterns that the child uses to mentally create a view of the world.

Equally important, researchers now know that emotions play a significant role in a child's attempts to find meaning in his experiences. The brain circuits that hold social and emotional experiences in memory are closely linked to the circuits that create meaning. How infants are held and taken care of; how often they are spoken to; the tone of voice, facial expressions, and eye contact used; and even the predictability and timing of adult responses to infants' needs all stimulate these parts of the brain.

From these experiences, infants create their first ideas or "opinions" of others, which create important patterns of excitement, evaluation, and response in the brain. These mental activities are essential to learning. We now know it is difficult to separate emotion, perception, and thinking, because they are nearly the same processes in the brain. Learning does not occur without emotion.

> *The brain circuits that hold social and emotional experiences are closely linked to the circuits that create meaning.*

Language Development

One of the most remarkable accomplishments of early childhood is learning language. From their earliest sounds, like crying, to their first attempts at words, infants begin to build a very complex communication system. During the first year, an infant is already focusing attention on other people, watching and gesturing at sources of sounds, connecting certain sounds and voices to particular events and people, trying to respond when talked to (when adult and infant coo back and forth to each other, for example), and learning to communicate needs and feelings.

From the moment of birth, infants seem to be "programmed" to communicate. They respond quickly to the sound of human voices, and they can tell the voice of their mother from other female voices. The different tones and patterns of infant crying communicate a variety of messages—hunger, discomfort, pain, anger, or boredom—messages that parents and other caregivers quickly learn to understand. Infants are also very social; they will stare at the faces of those who talk and sing to them, and they are sensitive to the emotional tone of their caregivers. Parents around the world adjust their speech styles when talking to infants, using the simplest words and exaggerating certain sounds and expressions, thus helping language develop.

Studies of early brain growth and neurological development suggest that a window of opportunity exists for the development of language. This period seems to happen during the first few months. During this time, opportunities to hear the language of others and observe its use in day-to-day interactions—and being gently talked and sung to—helps infants learn to understand their caregivers long before their brains develop enough for them to begin speaking.

Language Development in the First Year

Under normal circumstances, all infants learn language in a similar and predictable way. This seems to be true regardless of where they live or what culture they belong to. As with other areas of development, not all children learn language at the same speed. By the end of the first year, for example, a few children will speak in sentences while others use only one-word "sentences" that can be understood only by those who care for them regularly.

Table 10.1: The Language of Infancy (Birth to One Year): Prelanguage Speech and Communication

From birth to 4 months
Communicates through crying, fretting, and other reflex actions, such as coughing, burping, sneezing
Looks into the eyes of caregivers
Looks for and listens to voices
Begins to hear the difference between speech sounds
Becomes sensitive to the emotional tone of voices
Produces some vowel sounds
Smiles and laughs

From 4 to 8 months
"Plays" with voice and sound making
Appears to experiment with contrasts in loud and soft sounds, low- and high-pitched sounds
Can say some vowel sounds
Combines some vowel and consonant sounds and begins to babble
Says strings of the same sounds: "mamamama," "bababababa," "dadadadada"
Says strings of two or three different sounds, such as "dabagiba"
Tries to make and repeat the sounds of another person as though they're having a conversation
Points and gestures to communicate

From 8 to 12 months
Babbling begins to have the tone and changes in sound of "real" language
"Words" may be accompanied by body language cues, such as nodding, turning, or shaking the head; making eye contact; gesturing; and making exaggerated sounds
"Words" can take the form of expressing a need or desire, for example, asking for a bottle, refusing to interact or cooperate, asking to be held
Early real words emerge
Infant understands and imitates communication motions (bye-bye, throw a kiss, clapping)
Babbling and early words exist together for a time

Literacy Development

Literacy, the ability to read and write, has its roots in a number of infant experiences and sensations. Listening to and "talking" with others, paying attention to the sounds and rhythms of the voices and language of caregivers and others, watching the facial expressions of their caregivers, and staring at objects of interest are the first steps on the road to reading and writing.

Infants benefit from and enjoy chanting, rhyming, singing songs, playing games of peek-a-boo and pat-a-cake, and reading baby books with their parents and caregivers. Hearing the rich sounds of stories and songs is a valuable and enjoyable time for infants. Over time, they help infants become more and more interested in both talking and books.

BOOKS FOR VERY YOUNG INFANTS

Format

- Board books that can stand in the corner of the crib or on the floor in view range
- Colorful or black-and-white drawings
- Lead-free and nontoxic construction (including inks, adhesives, and paper or cardboard content)
- No small removable parts
- Rounded edges (no staples, spirals, or other sharp or detachable parts)

Content and illustrations

- Image of one simple object per page (point-and-say books)
- Familiar objects, such as baby bottle, soft stuffed toy, ball, cup, sweater, cap

BOOKS FOR OLDER INFANTS WHEN BOOKS CAN BE GRASPED, MOUTHED, AND HELD

Format

- Washable cloth books
- Washable soft plastic or vinyl books
- Lead-free and nontoxic construction (including inks, adhesives, and paper or cardboard content)
- No small removable parts
- Rounded or soft edges (no staples, spirals, or other sharp or detachable parts)

Content and illustrations

- More point-and-say books with a larger "vocabulary" of familiar objects or story content
- Touch-and-smell books
- Simple illustrations (avoid books with too many items in each drawing or on each page)
- Simple, one-word print labels together with pictures or drawings
- Simple, one-, two-, or three-line stories in which the story length and complexity increases little by little as the infants get older and are better able to pay attention

Factors Affecting Cognitive, Language, and Literacy Development

Think again about Jeremy and Angela. From the descriptions of their lives so far, it's easy to see that several factors influence their development in many areas. Let's compare their lives in terms of the factors that affect thinking and understanding, language, and literacy. Some of these factors include the following:

- Full-term infants get off to a healthier, less at-risk start in life. Being healthy from birth and having access to good health care help all development—physical and motor, psychological, social, cognitive, language, and literacy.
- Having good hearing and vision helps support and improve learning.
- Proper nutrition is essential to good health and to make the best brain and neurological development possible. Proper and adequate nutrition during the earliest months are critical for brain growth and neurological development. If malnutrition is severe during the first six months, the harmful effects can be permanent.
- Home and child care situations that support infants' cognitive, language, and literacy development with appealing social interaction, enriching stimulation, opportunities to explore their environment, and appropriate baby books and playthings all promote the best possible development.
- Interactions with other people who are responsive, supportive, and stimulating not only help infants' psychosocial development, but their thinking skills, language, and literacy development too.

Adults can assist and improve infant cognition, language development, and growing literacy in a number of ways. But development cannot be hurried. It is important that parents and other caregivers pay attention to the infant's own pace of development; in a sense, the infant should be their guide. Giving them too much stimulation, giving them toys that aren't appropriate, placing them in environments that are too busy or noisy, and in general expecting more than the infant is developmentally capable of doing can actually slow down their psychosocial and cognitive development. In confusing and overstimulating conditions, for example, infants become irritable, stressed, and sometimes depressed. They may also have problems eating, sleeping, paying attention, and playing.

Reference

Siegel, D. J. 1999. *The developing mind: Toward a neurobiology of interpersonal experience.* New York: Guilford.

The Role of the Early Childhood Professional

1. Interact often with infants and respond to their signals for social and emotional support.
2. Provide a rich social environment that includes opportunities for infants to watch, interact with, and be a part of the family or child care group.
3. Provide a safe, supportive, and nurturing environment that encourages exploration beyond the crib or playpen.
4. Provide a sensory-rich environment, including soft talking and singing, shared baby books, story reading, bright and cheerful surroundings, access to windows, simple, uncluttered pictures on the wall, and so on.
5. Provide an environment in which infants can talk and laugh with their caregivers and listen to singing, chanting, reading, taped music, and other sources of interesting sounds.
6. Provide objects infants can touch and play with, such as appropriate stuffed toys and other soft items.
7. Occasionally change what infants can view: Move the crib to another side of the room and change the art on the walls around the crib or play areas.
8. Provide safe, simple, interesting, age-appropriate toys and crib items, and change them when the infant loses interest in them.
9. Explore the surroundings with the infant, carrying her about, looking into mirrors, pointing to a photograph on the wall, looking through a window, and so on.
10. Take older infants on brief trips, such as to a store or a park. Talk about where you are going, what you are doing, and what you are seeing. Name objects, places, and people as you go.
11. Place older infants' toys on low, open shelves where they can reach them easily.
12. Respond with interest and enthusiasm when infants try to play with you or relate to you.

Discussion Questions

1. Piaget believed that young children think and solve problems quite differently than adults do. Name some examples from your observations that support this theory.
2. Based on observations of infants you've made, which of the four theories of cognitive development discussed in chapter 9 (cognitive/developmental, information processing, social/interactionist, and contextualist) do you feel has the most relevance to your own experiences? Which has the least relevance? Provide anecdotes from your experiences with infants that support your answers.

3. How do you help the infants in your care develop an interest in speaking and books? Based on what you've read, what are some examples of age-appropriate, preliteracy activities that you can do with infants? Conduct an online search or visit your local library to see what no-cost or low-cost materials are available to supplement your infant offerings.

4. Review the list titled "Role of the Early Childhood Professional." Does your program provide some or all of these opportunities and experiences for infants? What would you add to this list?

Further Reading

Bredekamp, S., and C. Copple, eds. 1997. *Developmentally appropriate practices in early childhood programs* (rev. ed.). Washington, D.C.: National Association for the Education of Young Children.

Byrnes, J. P. 2001. *Minds, brains, and learning: Understanding the psychological and educational relevance of neuroscientific research*. New York: Guilford Press.

Cryer, D., and T. Harms. 2000. *Infants and toddlers in out-of-home care*. Baltimore: P. Brookes.

Greenspan, S. I., and Beryl Lieff Benderly. 1997. *The growth of the mind: And the endangered origins of intelligence*. Reading, Mass.: Addison-Wesley.

Hast, F., and A. Hollyfield. 2001. *More infant and toddler experiences*. St. Paul, Minn.: Redleaf Press.

Neuman, S. B., C. Copple, and S. Bredekamp. 2000. *Learning to read and write: Developmentally appropriate practices for young children*. Washington, D.C.: National Association for the Education of Young Children.

Index

Other Resources from ![leaf] Redleaf Press